MICHEL FOUCAULT
AND THE POLITICS
OF FREEDOM

MODERNITY AND POLITICAL THOUGHT

Series Editor: Morton Schoolman
State University of New York at Albany

This unique collection of original studies of the great figures in the history of political and social thought critically examines their contributions to our understanding of modernity, its constitution, and the promise and problems latent within it. These works are written by some of the finest theorists of our time for scholars and students of the social sciences and humanities.

MICHEL FOUCAULT AND THE POLITICS OF FREEDOM

THOMAS L. DUMM

Modernity and Political Thought
VOLUME 9

ALTAMIRA
PRESS

A Divison of
ROWMAN & LITTLEFIELD PUBLISHERS, INC.
WALNUT CREEK • LANHAM • NEW YORK • OXFORD

ALTAMIRA PRESS
A Division of Rowman & Littlefield Publishers, Inc.
1630 North Main Street, # 367
Walnut Creek, CA 94596
http://www.altamirapress.com

Rowman & Littlefield Publishers, Inc.
4720 Boston Way
Lanham, MD 20706

12 Hid's Copse Road
Cumnor Hill, Oxford OX2 9JJ, England

British Library Cataloguing in Publication Information Available

Greater Kailash I
New Delhi 110 048 India

Printed in the United States of America

Library of Congress Cataloging-in-Publication Data

Dumm, Thomas L.
    Michel Foucault and the politics of freedom / author, Thomas L.
Dumm.
        p. cm. — (Modernity and political thought; vol.9)
    Includes bibliographical references and index.
        ISBN 0-8039-3864-0 (acid-free paper). — ISBN 0-8039-3865-9
pbk.: acid-free paper)
        1. Foucault, Michel—Contributions in political science.
2. Liberty. I. Title. II. Series.
JC261.F68D85   1996
320'.092—dc20   95-41747

    97 98 99 10 9 8 7 6 5 4 3 2

This book is printed on acid-free paper.

Sage Production Editor: Diana E. Axelsen
Sage Copy Editor: Joyce E. Kuhn
Sage Typesetter: Joe Cribben

*To Brenda Bright,
Irene Morning, and James Craft*

Because there was marriage there were children.
Because there were children, and fervor in the blood and brain,
books were born as well as daughters.

—Willa Cather,
The Professor's House

Contents

Series Editor's Introduction

Thomas Dumm's *Michel Foucault and the Politics of Freedom* is the ninth volume to appear in the Sage series **Modernity and Political Thought**. Dumm's work follows the 1994 publication of Stephen White's *Edmund Burke: Modernity, Politics and Aesthetics*; Tracy Strong's *Jean-Jacques Rousseau: The Politics of the Ordinary*; Jane Bennett's *Thoreau's Nature: Ethics, Politics and the Wild*; and George Kateb's *Emerson and Self-Reliance* (volumes 5 through 8, respectively). **Modernity and Political Thought** was inaugurated in 1993 with the publication of William Connolly's *The Augustinian Imperative: A Reflection on the Politics of Morality*, Richard Flathman's *Thomas Hobbes: Skepticism, Individuality and Chastened Politics*; Fred Dallmayr's *G. W. F. Hegel: Modernity and Politics*; and Michael Shapiro's *Reading "Adam Smith": Desire, History and Value* (volumes 1 through 4). The series will continue with books on selected past political thinkers by leading contemporary political theorists. These will include studies of Hannah Arendt by Seyla Benhabib, Sigmund

Freud by Jean Elshtain, and Friedrich Nietzsche by Benjamin Barber. As those who are familiar with the previous works of these authors will expect, these studies adopt a variety of approaches and pose importantly different questions. As contributors to **Modernity and Political Thought,** however, their efforts also are commonly devoted to examining the contributions that major political theorists have made to our understanding of modernity —its constitution and the problems, promises, and dangers that are latent within it.

Thomas Dumm's work has made important strides toward the clarification of the political contours of power—power rooted in its relations to knowledge—that in poststructuralism and postmodernism appear to fall outside the boundaries of what conventionally is understood to be "political." For political and social theorists whose points of departure for thinking about power are pre-Nietzschean, the political is elusive if not invisible if it loses its Hobbesian or Hegelian associations with the state, as it does in poststructuralist and postmodernist thought. Dumm's clarifications reveal the extent to which power that is unequivocally political insinuates itself into each and every facet of our existence, so much so that it is no longer meaningful to speak of a separation of public and private that exempts any sphere of life from the invasions of political power. In light of Dumm's work, we might say that power, specifically political power, actually is *productive* of life.

This last point emerges unavoidably from Dumm's insights into the political qualities of power relations as they are conceptualized by poststructuralism and postmodernism. It is especially important, for it opens to the problem that is the focus of *Michel Foucault and the Politics of Freedom.* The omnipresence of political power relations that, as the agency that surreptitiously lies behind or within all other agents, is productive of life in each of its forms presses us to raise a question that was unimaginable at the birth of the Enlightenment. In what ways can we yet think of ourselves as free subjects where "rights" are the expressions of our autonomy and the architectural tools of our existence rather than vehicles through which we unwittingly become dominated by those very relations in which our freedom and rights made it possible to become implicated? What, in other words, might be the alternative to disciplinary society? For Dumm, whose thinking about politics and power, freedom, and rights has been guided by Foucault, this was the issue that arose dramatically in the wake of his first book, *Democracy and Punishment,* where he was so taken by the way in which the form of society that most explicitly developed a regime of rights also most tightly conformed, in its genealogy, to the formal emergence of disciplinary society.[1] So closely do democracy and discipline accord, that the invention and perfection of the penitentiary by a democratic order ceases in any way to be discontinuous with democracy's deepest aspirations. With Dumm's study, democratic institutions and practices seemed to foreclose on the possibility of alternatives to disciplinary order not by failing but—ironically—by succeeding to do precisely what they were designed to do.

In much the same way as in *Democracy and Punishment,* the problem of freedom continued to shadow Dumm's next and relentlessly provocative work, *united states.*[2] Here his overall intent is to determine whether the play of desire in political life contributes to the creation of a disciplinary order to the exclusion of any possibilities for reinvigorating democratic life. In what uncommon ways, Dumm asks, are public representations and displays of political power rooted in the desires of those who hold office? And as uncommon expressions of intensely personal desires, do these same public representations and displays of political power draw out elements of popular desire by stimulating our own most private images of power, of personal and collective security, and even of resentment of those who hold powerful political positions? Are democratic politics after all only a politics of the desires within each of us? Do our desires belie the quest for democracy precisely because it, like the desires that may rule us with the force of law, is so deeply embedded in our American psyche?

The implications of Dumm's approach quickly become apparent. By tying political power to the reservoirs of human desire and to a democratic project that involves each of us in its political process, Dumm fathoms democracy's perhaps limitless potential for order. Can desire transform freedom into such a wellspring for a bondage that becomes our fundamental united state? Must placing the possibility of freedom under such enormous pressure be the inevitable consequence of an approach loyal to genealogical investigation? Is freedom finally excluded by the methodological *disciplines* we learn from Foucault? Is freedom simply unthinkable if we think with Foucault?

It is not difficult to understand how such expert genealogical analysis as Dumm's can force these types of questions upon the theorist with great urgency. Considering a few of the arguments in *united states* will illustrate my point. "The arrangements of power we find most appropriate in our united states," Dumm proposes, "are continuous with whom we love and how we love: our core love is for men in the superior position."[3] Dumm is not speaking figuratively, as though he had in mind the ordinary citizen who, casually expressing approval of a proposed tax cut, speaks lovingly of a politician. Rather, he is pointing to the attachments incited by our most special desires, those private codes of desire that may form our public choices, where desire may follow laws of its own and all other laws may follow from the law of desire.

Dumm offers us a particularly brutal example of the subterranean ties between politics and desire and its consequences. John Henry Abbott achieved fame after his release from prison through the publication of his prison letters and also for his subsequent conviction of manslaughter for the murder of Richard Adan, an aspiring actor and night manager of a New York City restaurant. Earlier, Abbott began a correspondence with Norman Mailer that described life within a maximum security prison, eventually producing *In the Belly of the Beast,* a book to which Mailer contributed a preface. Mailer's preface, Dumm argues, introduces less the thought of Abbott than the code of desire that Mailer understands to fuel our system of justice. The connections that Dumm traces between laws that imprison and the violence, especially sexual violence, that inmates suffer convey how desire is inscribed in the normal structure of political power. Dumm's reasons for looking to the example of prison life are twofold. Prison life is an arena not only where the relationship between political power and desire is visible and explicit but also where the violence entailed by the power relation between politics and desire is uncovered. At the same time, by making the relationship between political power and desire transparent, Dumm enables us to be sensitive to the more subtle ties between political power and desire in the public arenas where it is concealed from view.

We might say that Dumm forces the relationship between politics and desire out of the closet. Roy Cohn, an attorney who made his living and reputation accusing others of politically betraying the United States government, among other of his positions worked as legal counsel to Senator Joseph McCarthy "exposing" people as members of the Communist Party. Despite his own relations with men, Dumm points out, Cohn maintained a lifelong public posture against homosexuality and gay rights and never confessed to his own sexual identity. In this context, however, what becomes most interesting and important about Cohn is what he did admit to—to finding politics his primary source of sexual pleasure. After citing remarks by Cohn to this effect, Dumm concludes,

> Why not find the very *idea* of American politics sexually stimulating? After all, politics for [Cohn], as a man in the superior position, is no more and no less than the exercise of desire. It finds its most salient expression in the play of exchange, in one hand washing the other, in the winning and losing that occurs between men. Cohn operated under a code that Sidney Zion, his authorized biographer, describes as favors given and favors received.[4]

The ties between political power and desire that Cohn betrays are reproduced at a higher level in the case of J. Edgar Hoover, Cohn's protector. Hoover, who developed the policing policies that would ensure that men like Jack Henry Abbott were the captured targets of sexual violence, Dumm recalls, publicly denounced homosexuality while engaging secretly in homosexual relations as had Cohn. Hoover's denunciations were justified by a moral and political discourse that neatly differentiated between filth and cleanliness, which he marshaled in his wars against social change in any and every area of social life. Whether it had to do with race relations and the acquisition of rights, the evolution of the family structure or the appearance of organized crime, social change soiled the world of right and wrong. As Dumm explains, Hoover's belief that the civil rights movement was in some ways worse than communism, in that it presented a challenge to the law that was graphically enacted, was buoyed by his judgments of Martin Luther King, Jr. To Hoover, King's sexual peccadilloes were "the most salient reflection of the general moral degeneracy of the entire civil rights movement, because they represented someone who was more than willing to live out ambivalent desires. Such inconsistency was for Hoover a simple sign of filth."[5]

Cohn and Hoover are but two of the representatives of a vicious politics that disguises the violence of the desires of its puritan practitioners, as Dumm proves clearly. Dumm's analysis of presidential politics also exemplifies—as in Bush's erstwhile campaign against AIDS or the humiliations to which he subjected foreign enemies or in the national debate about gay men in the military—the ways in which the politics of desire extends beyond those in superior positions and taps into and nurtures deeply held popular prejudices about homosexuality. The campaign against "queer-ness," as Dumm puts it, from the "very top to the very bottom" is a united state that contributes to perpetuating established political and personal identities, the beliefs, hopes, and fears of its leaders and citizens alike. Yet this campaign is only one of the myriad forms that the code of desire assumes in politics and that turns democratic practices into a dupe of the sexual desires that Freud once referred to as "eternal forces."

Does Dumm's work not allow us to speak of a conspiracy between politics and desire, an uninterrupted conspiracy that protects the superior positions of men in power while at the same time preserving the superiority—over women, racial minorities, and gays—of the more ordinary men whose own desire provides popular support for the politically powerful? But does this conspiracy not also function to imprison the conspirators as well as the victims of the conspiracy, the masters as well as the slaves? This second question points to the more subtle dimensions of the relationship between politics and desire only hinted at thus far and ones not less vicious for their subtlety. It points ever more sharply, too, to an explanation for how Dumm's genealogical analyses led him to suspect the precariousness of the concept of freedom. In what new senses are conspirators and their victims imprisoned?

An answer is provided by Dumm's examination of the Rodney King beating and the verdict that acquitted the officers for the crime and precipitated the 1992 riots in Los Angeles. How, Dumm considers, did the members of the jury in Simi Valley reach their verdict to acquit the police who brutalized Rodney King? Had they simply succumbed to racial fears and, motivated by an atavistic terror of the unknown, are they nothing more than racial bigots? If so, had the jurors wished through their verdict to send the message that the authorities must be permitted to beat black men who act suspiciously, especially outside their own neighborhoods?

While Dumm does not entirely discount this sort of explanation, he is unwilling to lay the blame simply or exclusively on hatred. To do so would risk overlooking other factors that might be importantly at work. Dumm focuses on forms of knowledge, specifically criminological discourses that divide populations into the normal and the pathological, which contribute to buttressing myths about the "abnormality" of minorities and to fortifying an interpretive framework for criminalizing "otherness." Along these lines, Dumm takes up a latter-day descendent of the scientific racism traceable to social Darwinism, James Q. Wilson and Richard Herrnstein's *Crime and Human Nature*, which he shows manufactures a theory of biological inferiority where statistical probability is used to verify claims about racial inferiority.[6] (It may be noted that Herrnstein went on to coauthor the controversial *Bell Curve*, a study that correlates intelligence with race.) Because the incidence of certain forms of criminal behavior correlates with membership in particular races, more specifically with being members of particular races who possess particular body types, statistically, its argument goes, those races are more likely to commit certain crimes. As Dumm explains, in this study and in others resembling it, race becomes a marker associated with a collection of social phenomena. The attachments of race to the body, to physical racial characteristics, are not established according to a logic of strict causality but alternatively through a logic of statistically valid correlation. Race becomes a "normalizing category" by using a shorthand of visible bodily markers to articulate its distinctiveness. In light of these types of "scientific" arguments offered by Wilson and Herrnstein, in other words, it becomes "statistically reasonable" to believe that anyone fitting Rodney King's profile—black, male and, at least in this case, an "endomorphic mesomorph"—harbors violent proclivities and is predisposed to commit violent crimes. The overall impact of such thinking is to shift our attention from "accountability for specific acts to response to predictable populations." Dumm draws a rather startling conclusion.

> King's responsibility extends not only to what he does, but to who he is. His body informed on him to the police. Even in its inability to be perfectly still, King's body showed the police that he was dangerous. . . . When they develop this sort of racist representational schema, contemporary criminologists move the categorization of the dangerous individual to a new level. Even if the criminal does not speak on his own behalf, even if his motives are not explained by investigation and confession, the body of the criminal itself speaks the "truth" of the criminal's character.[7]

To put this insight into the simplest possible terms, Rodney King looks like someone who would commit a crime! He falls out of the range of "normality." And those who are within the range of the normal, who are not "statistically" threatening, are quite likely to be anxious at the mere presence of a Rodney King in their neighborhoods not only because they worry about him but because his presence calls into question their normality as well. Likewise, the police could be held to be entirely justified in having savaged Rodney King, whose appearance warrants the harshest treatment. Hence the verdict of a jury who confused reality with the politics of appearance.

It is easy to see that the process of normalization that is here assisted by social scientific discourse constitutes boundaries that are not only conceptual. Indeed, while at the theoretical level firm distinctions are being drawn between the normal and abnormal, moral and immoral, law abiding and deviant or criminal, at the level of practice, that is, at the level of ordinary, everyday life, equally firm lines are being drawn between those who belong and those who are strangers, between friends and enemies, between those who look the same and those who are different. This normalization process reconstitutes the community as an "enclosed space." The world outside the familiar surroundings of the (normalized) community is dangerous; safety lies only within. These "new enclosures," as Dumm describes them, therefore confine those who "do belong" as much as they exclude those who "do not belong." Normalization separates and excludes, but it also "interns." No one escapes incarceration, no one is "free," neither the imprisoned black man nor the white who is confined to the comfortable surroundings of the suburban carceral. Freedom disappears from the territory inhabited by the normal no less than it is absent from the territory inhabited by the deviant, a territorialization that begins with the threatening body of the black and spreads to the threatened body of the white.

Dumm's analysis of the politics of desire leads him to a consideration of the politics of space, a new context within which he is able to outline the parameters of the problematic of freedom in late modernity even more precisely. Although we might think that our feelings of *being at home* would parallel the extent to which the environments in which we live, work, and travel become "new enclosures," these safe and predictable reservations cause a certain vertigo or disorientation. As more and more that surrounds us is secured and begins to look alike, "everything looks familiar but nothing looks *definite*."[8] If we appear to belong everywhere, Dumm is suggesting, the certainty about where we really belong is eroded, perhaps lost. In the midst of the familiarity bred by the new enclosures, in other words, we become disoriented. The boundaries of our identities, distinguishing who we are and what we are in terms of where we are *not,* are dissolved in a new spatiality that does not differentiate, that undermines differentiation. The "new enclosures," initially returning that sense of place and security threatened by those demons conjured up through the processes of normalization, incite a homesickness that spurs the quest for a home within each of us. This quest for the *certainty* of a home is poisonous, Dumm explains eloquently, because

> democracy is connected to a form of homelessness, in that it requires that one *overcomes* the desire to be at home. Home, in our contemporary democracy, is comprehended as a private place, a place of withdrawal from the demands of common life, a place of fixed meaning where one is protected from disorientation, but also from the possibility of democratic involvement. Hence one might say that democratic life requires one to overcome the fear of homelessness, to develop the courage to leave home (embracing another fear) without knowing when or whether one will return.[9]

Can we, Dumm is intimating, recover the idea of homelessness as a way to think about the American democratic condition, as a way to develop a critical perspective on the enclosures within which we are becoming locked? How might homelessness, which has done so much to disable us, become a philosophical and political asset?

For Dumm there is far more at stake in the problem of homelessness, then, than humanitarians have led us to understand. Dumm's claim that democracy requires that one develop the courage to leave the privacy and security of home to become oriented toward a public life that contests the fixity of who we are and what we believe establishes a connection between homelessness and freedom. Are the homeless perhaps those who find oppressive, Dumm is asking, the circumstances that govern organized, normalized life? Are the homeless not seeking out alternatives, desperate ways to live outside the containment fields that circumscribe modern experience and fix our identities? Do the homeless articulate a desire in each of us to disappear, to become anonymous and thus escape the new enclosures?

If there is such a connection between homelessness and freedom, the way in which America struggles with homelessness is tied dangerously not only to the issue of whether the United States is humane but to whether it will oppose enclosure. Indeed, Dumm is proposing that when we frame homelessness as an issue of freedom, rather than in terms of whether the needs of a mass of unfortunates are being met, the "condition" of the homeless suggests that we are suffering an emergency of freedom. Put bluntly, enclosure may have become so fundamental and universal that homelessness appears as the only way to escape it, escape its agoraphobic politics of identity and the erasure of freedom that this politics entails for those interned on the inside *or* on the outside. In essence, Dumm is arguing, America's struggle with homelessness is tied intimately to whether it will remain a democracy. Dumm powerfully conveys the sense in which American democratic life depends on the united state of homelessness replacing our united state of security.

As has been painfully obvious, however, especially during the Reagan and Bush years, America's struggle with homelessness has taken the form of a struggle against the homeless. Laws are passed that increasingly deprive the homeless of the space to satisfy their most basic human needs and wants. With increasing restrictions and regulations, all public places where the homeless can be at home eventually will disappear. By driving the homeless out of sight, homelessness is driven out of mind. And when along with the homeless the idea of homelessness vanishes, a provocative representation of the idea of freedom, one that urges hostility toward enclosure, vanishes as well. When framed as an issue of freedom, Dumm concludes, the specter of the homeless and the militant remedies for homelessness indicate that we are suffering an emergency of freedom. The urgency to make homelessness go away reflected in public policies on the homeless may be a measure of how universal containment has become. Accordingly, Dumm reasons, the homeless serve as a type of monitor for us.

Can we integrate the homeless into our lives, homelessness into our thinking? The homeless would remind us of the freedom missing from our own lives, make us aware of the enclosures within which we live, suggest what distances we must travel in order to step outside our identities. But even if we could integrate the homeless and homelessness, are they not on the margins of our experience and the lessons that homelessness teaches only on the margins of our thought? More generally, how can we move freedom from the margins into the center of an existence that has shut it out as it has shut us in? It is to this task that Dumm's work has led him, and to which he now turns in *Michel Foucault and the Politics of Freedom.*

With the publication of Volume 9 of the series, Carrie Mullen is leaving **Modernity and Political Thought** and Sage Publications. Carrie will be greatly missed by all those who have contributed to this series, and she has our appreciation for an excellence that helped to make each of its volumes successful. Our thanks also go to Diana Axelsen for editorial talents that consistently bring out the series' best qualities and to Abby Nelson for picking up where Carrie left off.

—*Morton Schoolman*
State University of New York at Albany

Notes

1. Thomas L. Dumm, *Democracy and Punishment: Disciplinary Origins of the United States* (Madison: University of Wisconsin Press, 1987).

2. Thomas L. Dumm, *united states* (Ithaca, NY: Cornell University Press, 1994).

3. Ibid, 49.

4. Ibid., 74.

5. Ibid., 76.

6. James Q. Wilson and Richard Herrnstein, *Crime and Human Nature* (New York: Simon & Schuster, 1985).

7. Dumm, *united states,* 103.

8. Ibid., 153 (emphasis added).

9. Ibid., 155 (emphasis added).

Preface

L et us invent a philosopher, pretend to discover her manuscripts in a cave somewhere, and come up with a pseudonym for her. Let's call her Michele Foucault. Around this nonexistent person we will be able to form opinions, around the constellations of work provided by our fictional being we will be able to set sail toward safe harbors . . . or stormy seas. The convenience of the name will make our otherwise tedious work quicker—we will coin new adjectives, such as Foucaultian, that will lend themselves to the task. This imaginary philosopher will be very useful to us in other ways as well. We will be able to oppose or support her, condemn or praise her, slander her or deify her, in turn, and should we be very inventive we might even do all these things simultaneously. In short, we should be able to do almost all the things that we do now with other thinkers of our own invention to avoid having to think for ourselves about our condition.

This substitute for thinking for ourselves is a remarkably enduring institution in the modern academy. It indicates a strong and persistent, if too rarely enunciated, faith that most of us have in the coherence and unity of individual lives: It reflects how we rely on such constructed unities to aid us through our own lives. At a less important level, the pastime of inventing philosophers—not usually out of whole cloth but through the constant activity of reinterpretation and partial appropriation of the works of specific individuals—contributes to building a canon and thus helps people get tenure at colleges and universities. Me too. Wittingly or unwittingly, simply by expressing myself within the institutional framework of the contemporary academy, I contribute to building a canon and to fetishizing those I have hoped I was only thinking with, adding to the construction of the official objects of power/knowledge within the modern academy. Generally, I believe that it is too bad that our circumstances make it difficult to evade this process. There are really too many books out there, and I worry that this one might be just another one. And while I suppose that writing about a particular thinker is not necessarily a completely useless or harmful exercise, sometimes I think it is too often confused with the companionship one gets from thinking with certain writers.

In the case of the thinker I have written about in this volume, a greater sensitivity than usual is probably called for. Michel Foucault cherished a particular kind of anonymity, largely as a reflection of his thinking about the various relationships that might hold between the constitution of self and the development of a particular regime of power/knowledge. Within our civilization, he sought to problematize the easy attachment of truth to authorship. As he put it in an interview, "A name makes reading too easy."[1] Foucault also reserved for himself certain thinkers, especially Nietzsche and Heidegger, as authors with whom he might have an intimate relationship. He sought to preserve his relationship to them by not writing about them. In his final interview, he said, "I think it is important to have a small number of authors with whom one thinks, with whom one works, but about whom one does not write. Perhaps I will write about [Nietzsche and Heidegger] someday, but at such a time they will no longer be instruments of thought for me."[2] Because Foucault remains an instrument of thought for me, the struggle I have had in writing this book has not been limited to or even importantly informed by the usual mundane distractions that afflict acknowledgment pages of academic books throughout the academy.

(Those of us who are likely to read books such as this one are now intimately familiar with, say, my long-suffering spouse, my demonic/distracting children whom I must promise never to neglect again, my supportive life companion to whom I owe everything, my dog, my cat, my parents, my siblings, my gastroenterologist. Again, me too. As the dedication of this book indicates, I'm a *family* person, just like so many others who have written about Foucault.) No, for me Foucault is the distraction that made this book difficult for me to write. Because his authorship is compelling to me, I continue to think with him, and thinking itself is, among other things, dis-tracting, a process of removing the pieties of the unthought from their tract so that they might be considered otherwise.

So we are presented with a paradox that is not resolvable but is, perhaps instead, negotiable. If one wants to think about Foucault, it is best to attend directly to his authorship. But because his authorship includes a critique of authorial authority, we might be encouraged to try instead to think with him rather than simply to follow him. This is a struggle, a pedagogical struggle, in which the authority of Foucault conflicts with his critique of authorship. I have tried to negotiate this paradox by engaging my much less considerable talents to thinking about an element of Foucault's work and mediating it through the concerns that most centrally occupy my thoughts. These concerns circle primarily around how we might be free when it seems as though the primary framework for being free in the modern age of Western capitalist democracies, that provided by liberal rights and democratic participation, is losing it grip on the imagination of the citizens of the world. My concerns are thus more parochial than Foucault's and certainly less completely articulated. But hopefully through the lens they provide, we might gain a better way to think for ourselves about how we might be free.

* * *

Morton Schoolman, the general editor of this series, has my thanks for both his editorial acumen and his extraordinary patience in waiting for a manuscript long overdue. Mort was especially helpful during the endless spring of 1995. Among those who have aided me in the process of thinking about Foucault, I am pleased to acknowledge the help of Jane Bennett, Roger Berkowitz, Wendy Brown, Jay Caplan, William Chaloupka, Shin Chiba, Barbara Cruikshank, James Der Derian, Frederick Dolan, Kathy Ferguson, Alex Hooke, Thomas Keenan, Laura Kurgan, Diane Rubenstein, Michael Shapiro, Stephen White, and Linda Zerilli for conversations about Foucault over the past years. Several friends took time and effort to comment on drafts of this manuscript. Richard Flathman and George Kateb provided me with their respective insights concerning what I would call (but they never would) tribal matters in liberal political thought and on general matters of scholarship and writing. Robert Gooding-Williams helped me understand Nietzsche better. Austin Sarat insisted that I think more about Isaiah Berlin. Bonnie Honig read with care several of the chapters, making valuable editorial suggestions, some of which I have incorporated, more of which I should have. Brenda Bright helped keep this work grounded by ensuring that it would not overtake other pleasures and by insisting that I connect theory to practice. William E. Connolly has once again added to my ever-growing debt to him; hopefully I'll someday have both the muscles and brains to carry that weight.

Notes

1. See "The Masked Philosopher," in Lawrence D. Kritzman, ed., *Michel Foucault: Politics, Philosophy, Culture* (New York: Routledge, 1988), 324. This interview was conducted under conditions of anonymity.
2. Michel Foucault, "Final Interview," trans. Thomas Levin and Isabelle Lorenz, *Raritan* 1 (Summer 1985): 9.

1

The Politics of Freedom

My role—and that is too emphatic a word—is to show people that they are much freer than they feel. . . . To change something in the minds of people— that is the role of the intellectual.

—"Truth, Power, Self: An Interview"

In a lecture he gave toward the end of his life Michel Foucault commented, "The failure of the major political theories nowadays must lead not to a nonpolitical way of thinking but to an investigation of what has been our political way of thinking during this century."[1] In this late lecture, Foucault gave fresh expression to a concern that animated all of his work. Foucault was curious about and concerned by what he saw as a distinctively modern impulse. Ironically, this impulse is inspired by, if not

Epigraph taken from an interview with Michel Foucault, in *Technologies of the Self: A Seminar with Michel Foucault,* ed. Luther Martin et al. (Amherst: University of Massachusetts Press, 1988), p. 35.

always explicitly enunciated within, political thought as the desire to escape from politics. For him, the escape from politics most importantly is to be understood as an escape from thinking through the limits of who we are, so as to learn how to be otherwise. Foucault was aware that such a desire for escape is inscribed in any search for "a nonpolitical way of thinking," but he also believed that it takes on an added urgency in the contemporary era. Marxist utopians, liberal privatists, communitarian theologians, utilitarian positivists, procedural democrats, communicative ethicists, fascist nationalists—for Foucault, the advocates of these various political projects share in the paradoxical quest to evade politics by making politics a means toward ends that are decidedly unpolitical. The normative claims advanced by partisans of the various ways of life that extend from their antipolitical visions are, in the end, unified in their search for a place of peace, a desire to place life's meaning outside of the struggles constitutive of politics. They all are willing to reduce politics itself to the rationality of policy or the irrationality of violence. In their willingness to reduce politics to a means, the advocates of modern evasions of the political, in an ironic twist, seem to repudiate the very means which enable them to constitute a space beyond politics.

Foucault's work confronts modern political thought in almost all of its guises, seeking a counterimpulse toward politics resting within the heart of modernity itself. As Jürgen Habermas noted in an uncharacteristically poetic turn upon Foucault's death, he took aim at the heart of the present.[2] But his approach was hardly direct and unambiguous. He sought what we might call the floating positions that could lead us toward a different way of thinking politically. From his genealogical perspective, he was able to characterize this century especially as an important transitional era in the history of attempts to evade politics, a century that has made visible, through new forms of war and through the invention of new kinds of murder, the potentially apocalyptic consequences of the various political projects of evading politics. We moderns—he is referring to "*our* political way of thinking"—are caught up in a quest to escape the world we have made. Yet, as Foucault knew better than most, each attempt we have made to escape our world has intensified our world's hold on us.

This paradox concerning the unresolvable character of political existence itself informs the trajectory of Foucault's thought and may make intelligible what sometimes seems to be a set of contradictory postures he has taken regarding political matters. For Foucault, politics is deeply bound up with the truths we construct in a given era, and the politics of truth is inevitably tied to the specific character of power/knowledge exhibited within any historically placed culture. But in all its complexity, the work of Foucault is nonetheless united in its ethos. For rather than seek one more escape, Foucault consistently looked for new ways to make the world habitable.

This book is premised on the notion that in seeking to make the world habitable Foucault enunciates a new political theory of freedom, one that relocates freedom within the realm of politics and in so doing redefines politics as an activity of self-constitution. Friedrich Nietzsche, perhaps Foucault's most important predecessor, developed his philosophical insights from within a relatively unproblematized space which allowed his concerns to be governed by the politics of friendship more than the politics of democracy. Nietzsche was not concerned with the ethics of the demos and did not seem worried about the capacity of most people to realize a freedom of action. Nietzsche believed that the overcoming of nihilism, which he understood as the necessary next step in the human overcoming of humanness, would be limited to a few and seemed unconcerned by the restrictions that would follow from the aristocratic politics he endorsed.

Foucault did not share Nietzsche's aristocratic perspective. His redefinition of politics can in part be apprehended as an attempt to democratize the great Nietzschean insights concerning power and nihilism. Such a democratization might make available to everyone and anyone the knowledge that it takes to come to act in this world with an awareness not of the extent of our enthrallment but of how we are indebted—to the past, to each other, to ourselves. It would allow us to understand more fully how a human history of indebtedness in the forms of guilt, bad conscience, and their ilk that developed, as Nietzsche taught, through a mnemonics of pain, informs the matrix of power and resentment that shapes our subjectivities. It also would make available to everyone the deep knowledge of the impact that the death of God has on the human prospect, a matter crucial to the overcoming of the cruelties and violences that currently shape our political contests. Implicit in such a project is a hope that with such knowledge it may yet be possible to avert a looming catastrophe in the history of humanity, one that threatens the future of existence itself.

If we imagine him as a philosopher of freedom, we might see that Foucault takes for his starting point the problematical status of freedom's contemporary existence as a sort of resistance to politics. Freedom is experienced as a recourse to and idealization of a variety of imaginary primal human situations—peace, desire, exchange, consumption—or any other human eventuality that might be construed to exist as an experience outside of politics. Because freedom stands as the empty space within which these experiences unfold, supposedly as a pure negativity, as an absence of resistance, freedom achieves a respect and admiration in the world of contemporary political life. It must be respected because without it those things that are most distinctly of human value cannot come to be, and it must be admired for the aesthetic experiences it supports and sustains. But in an age when, as Foucault suggests, "politics places [man's] existence as a living being in question," the fate of the political itself is called into doubt if there is no way to situate freedom as coterminous with, rather than as opposed to, the space of politics.[3] That most attempts to comprehend the politics of freedom in the modern West have been fated to understand freedom itself as a kind of absence or to locate it in the interior experience of those who bear its mark so as to disappear from reasoned consideration suggests to Foucault a need to reassert freedom's presence in the infra- structure of political life itself. How freedom as an experience is to be expressed in the face of the new enclosures that have been constructed around it in order to control the conditions of its expression is a dangerous and difficult matter. It is made so because the resentment of those whose self-understanding includes the need to maintain a *security* of self by rejecting an openness to others is exacerbated to the extent that their claims for the privilege of their protected freedom, freedom as a product of enclosure, are challenged.[4]

Liberals, Marxists, New Manicheans

Indeed, those who oppose the politicization of freedom can find in the thought of Foucault much that is dangerous. Liberals have a deep concern that the investigations pursued by Foucault are themselves a threat to what is a remarkable and positive achievement, the spread of a way of being free that enables entire polities to live freely through institutions that establish the rights of citizenship for all. The freedom espoused by liberals is especially congruent with the institutionalization of the rights that provide the framework of freedom, and much is risked when the idea of freedom as right is challenged. While it remains a matter of argument whether the history of liberal freedom has been as remarkable a historical success as its advocates suggest, especially given the tremendous costs associated with its realization, that argument must nevertheless be considered in a comparative context.[5] From the perspective of most liberals, the bulk of Foucault's work has participated in damaging the faith in liberal freedom necessary for its continued sustenance as a value and its effective operation within institutions.

I find in the work of some liberals much food for thought regarding this critique of Foucault. Indeed, I would agree with them when they note that the political themes developed by Foucault might most fruitfully be pursued in reference to, if not from within, existing liberal frameworks for understanding freedom.[6] But unlike these liberals, I would argue that such an engagement cannot proceed as though the current vocabulary of liberalism can remain unchanged. The language of liberalism has adhered to a straightforwardness, born of a desire for universalism and timelessness that it can no longer sustain. The path to an engagement with Foucault's thought of freedom is not necessarily through a rehabilitation of the subject created and sustained by liberal civilization. That subject, the democratic individual, is for traditional liberals the exclusive site of freedom. In decided contrast, freedom as developed in Foucault's thought is much stranger than even that strange product of modernity, the individual, and may best be thought about in the wake of an explicit acknowledgment of how the strategies of power in the late modern era have gravitated away from the individual subject, indeed, with the individual's continued existence as an object of political contestation called into doubt. For some, this acknowledgment has taken a strongly Heideggerian form. But Foucault, while indebted to Heidegger, takes his own distinctive path through the impasses of late modernity.

Other species of objection to Foucaultian freedom are posed by two alternative foundational critiques of late modernity. The first of these is neo-Hegelian, or more specifically, Marxist, in origin and sees the modern era as something that needs to be fulfilled through the progressive realization of social justice. Even in the wake of the failure of actually existing state socialism this realization still entails the overcoming of capitalism, which is understood as the organizational force of the last instance determining the ontological status of humans as alienated beings. Much of what contemporary Marxists see as valuable in Foucault's work concerns the sustained analysis of discipline he presents in *Discipline and Punish*. But that very analysis is both superfluous and absolutist from the perspective of late Marxism, in that it decenters the study of the conditions that would be necessary for "true" freedom to be realized as a product of revolution, the overcoming of the current conditions of social reproduction. Late capitalism and the concomitant intensification of commodification in late modernity have in turn made both the reading of those conditions and the prescriptions for revolutionary action quite different from their more classical formulations concerning the violent overthrow of capitalist states.[7] While the material terms through which revolutionary action is to be realized have mutated in late Marxism, underlying the argument of most of those who still adhere to a variant of Marxism is a Hegelian *telos* dependent on a utopian belief in the realization of social justice, one that does not sit well with the strongly anti-utopian conclusions entailed in Foucault's work.

As the Marxist critique has migrated into the field of identity politics in the past twenty years and as a variety of adherents to solid group identities have emerged to stake their various claims to the fragmented remnants of revolutionary ideologies, they have found in the work of Foucault a potent opposition. Revolutionary subjects get into trouble when the terms through which their constitution as such subjects are unveiled as the contingent products of forces that shape the very terms of their subjecthood. Hence, the style through which they might claim to liberate themselves, whether it be through a struggle to achieve community in opposition to others or through a struggle to overthrow the material conditions that brought them into existence as a subordinate class, is in both cases strongly influenced by a teleology of positive freedom. This freedom, in its solidification of identity and constriction of the possibility of imagining alternative styles of being, is vehemently opposed by Foucault.

The other foundational critique of late modernity—and the one that has the greatest cultural force at the end of the millennium in the United States—is that advanced by fundamentalist reactionaries of various persuasions. These moral absolutists, or new Manicheans, are united in their rejection of Enlightenment standards of truth, seeing in the various expressions of Enlightenment thought a relativism that is nihilistic at its core. They understand freedom itself to be dangerous, in that it ambiguates the codes of good and evil that are essential to their claims to solid identity. They argue that freedom is itself a form of license and that its spread to

large numbers is a sign of the nihilism of the modern age. Under the banner
of various command moralities, whether derived from the tenets of Christian fundamentalism, Catholicism, behavioralism and other social scientific "realisms," or Straussianism, these contemporary critics of freedom
comprehend the modern world as fallen and see freedom as a sensibility
that encourages subjects to express nihilistic evil.[8]

Throughout this book the most important conversation I will try to stage
is between Foucault and the proponents of liberal freedom and post-Marxist
theorists of community. At times, this conversation will overlap with other
conversations, but the primary effort here is to show the distinctive contribution Foucault makes to the philosophy of freedom, not to defend his
version of freedom against those who either secretly or openly question
freedom as a primary value.

Contextualizing Freedom

In presenting Foucault as a political theorist I am only building on work
that has been done by many others in the decade since Foucault's death.
But it might be useful for those who only recently have encountered the
work of Foucault, especially within the world of political theory, to be
reminded that the earlier trajectory of Foucault's work did not directly or
obviously lead to the line of inquiry I pursue here. It is, of course, a claim
of this book that there is a deep continuity in his work and that his concern
with subjectivity and, more specifically, with the genealogy of the modern
subject as an object of power is profoundly tied to the emergence of his
concerns as a political theorist. But while he had published pathbreaking
works on questions of marginalization, madness and reason, the medical
gaze, the history of science, and aesthetics, and while one might have been
able to discern a deep and provocative understanding of politics implicitly
in his earlier works, perhaps especially in *The Order of Things,* prior to the
1970s Foucault was most famous in France and in North America as a
structuralist historian who turned on structuralism, a philosopher of science
who concentrated on the least epistemologically secure of sciences (those
taking as their domain of inquiry aspects of human being), and a theorist
of literature who was concerned more with the anonymous inscriptions of

language than with the artistry of particular authors. Foucault himself did not seem immediately to understand how he was writing about power and politics in those early works. Especially for American audiences, less informed of the cultural politics that then so dramatically shaped (and it seems, continue to shape) the representation of French intellectual life, the Foucault who appeared before the events of May 1968 was not understood as a political thinker at all but as the writer of a dazzling, radical, and obscure study of the history of insanity, *Madness and Civilization*.

Foucault's reputation, especially in the Anglo-American world, underwent a significant change after the publication of *Discipline and Punish*. This study of what he ambitiously identified as "the birth of the prison" commanded the attention of almost all who study the history of political thought. Among other achievements, in *Discipline and Punish* Foucault shows why it is valuable to think about the power to punish crime in a new way: not as a marginal, albeit important, function of the modern state but as a register more generally of the meaning of modern politics in the West. This novel assertion concerning the meaning of punishment alone was explosive, and the explosion was perhaps even more intensely felt coming as it did from within the context of French culture, a culture that in its most important political commitments had, since long before the French Revolution, focused the study of power and politics almost exclusively on the activity of the modern state. Foucault's attention to the prison and his detailed descriptions of the dissemination of discipline beyond the state suggested that the arguments concerning justice advanced by those on the state-oriented left are severely flawed, in that they fail to address the multivalent ways in which power inscribes itself on individuals. That failure, Foucault was to argue, contributes mightily to perpetuating the conditions that those concerned with liberation should want to transform.

Foucault's critical analysis of what he termed disciplinary society was rooted in a Nietzschean understanding of how morality and justice are founded. And this innovation alone might have signaled something novel in the ongoing conversation of political thought. But Foucault's radically Nietzschean critique of arguments concerning justice was not the only way in which that book operated as a form of dynamite. His Nietzscheanism was both more extensive and intensive than that. Among other things, *Discipline and Punish* demonstrates that there is a history of ideas that escapes the sanctity of canonization by intellectual historians, a history that is in direct contrast to such canonization and is instead furiously relevant to the present. In the United States especially, those who taught political thought either as a tradition in the progressive realization of Enlightenment ideas or as its opposite, as the decline of the West, were to be both perplexed and infuriated by the radically contemporary quality of Foucault's excavation of the seemingly marginal practices of physiocrats and scientific cranks, placing their *practices* at the heart of the meaning of Enlightenment itself. That he did so in the name of understanding the heart of the present made it even more difficult to accept his analyses.

Obviously, Foucault (with other poststructuralists—and most important, although he engaged in deep and sometimes acrimonious controversy with him, Jacques Derrida) antagonized the various parties of political theory in part because throughout his career he was, to use the most common cliché, "fashionable." He became fashionable, which is most often simply an envious way to identify an important figure in the constellation of contemporary thought, in large part because his work appealed to younger scholars less tethered to arguments within the academy between the aging members of the American New Left and their liberal and conservative counterparts. Foucault provided a way to move beyond the impasse of the main camps in American political theory, namely, the liberals and communitarians. Foucault was not a conservative but more accurately could be characterized as a "Left-Nietzschean," to recall William E. Connolly's useful phrase.[9] Part of the reason why his genealogies startled so many people is not only because they challenged the domination of a particular kind of political theory but because they traced an element of the truth of the practices of political theory as a thread of the modern will to power, that which expresses itself in the constitution of our most convenient truths. Because the political theories upon which the liberal, conservative, and the early communitarian camps rested were, by the late 1970s, firmly entrenched as the arbiters of the relationship of theory to truth, having basically survived the challenge presented within political science by the rise of behavioralism in the post-World War II era, Foucault's work operated as an offense to all who functioned within the settled terms of political discourse.[10]

In the United States, the publication of *Discipline and Punish* served as well to introduce the thought of Nietzsche to a younger generation of students of political thought. Most of these younger scholars had not yet been exposed to the way in which Nietzsche might be relevant to contemporary political problems. Indeed, a large measure of the influence of that book (as well as the power of much of Foucault's work) has stemmed from its exemplary ability to develop Nietzschean themes concerning will, truth, and power, making them painfully relevant to the most contemporary political concerns. Foucault's work provided a fresh link to the political concerns that animated so much contemporary discussion of politics—social justice, equality, freedom, and the structural barriers to the achievement of all of these. At the same time, it served as a harsh repudiation of the pieties of so many who thought that their own political motives are pure, by demonstrating the ways in which the premises of their political commitments themselves operate as means of domination.

Moreover, in the wake of the high water mark of the antiwar and civil rights movements, issues concerning sexual identity, social order and disorder, and the ways in which authority operates in modernity so as to evade responsibility for its most troubling effects, namely, the persistence of state power, came to the fore in discussions within the engaged intellectual left but without the sort of vocabulary that would enable the participants in these microstruggles to understand *how* the personal is political. Foucault provided a framework for understanding these struggles.[11] They grew primarily out of the social and political upheavals of the previous decades not only in the United States but throughout the world. The breakup of the colonial world order and the rise of new forms of imperialism, the rise of the civil rights movement and violent resistance to social equality, the emergence of a youth culture as a counterculture, the appearance of the contemporary women's movement as a refiguring of the very location where power is most decisively defined and struggled over, and the emergence of a gay liberation movement that calls into question the very terms of gender identity were not, as some conservative critics would have it, the results of an academic conspiracy.[12] Instead, because the genre of social changes in the outside world concerned issues of representation, social transformation, and other contestations of culture, the academy, as a repository of information about these matters, became a condensation site of struggle, a place of the world but not quite in it, where the world's turmoil found and continues to find intellectual voice.

Prior to Foucault, the issue of the relevance of political thought to action had been most decisively undertaken by scholars most closely associated with the Frankfurt School. In the American academy, the gradual canonization of the work of such Frankfurt School luminaries as Adorno, Horkheimer, Marcuse, and, to a lesser extent, Benjamin might be seen as the result of their persistent concern to express the conflict between theory and practice. In many ways, their work, especially that of Marcuse, served as midwife to the birth of a New Left or at least that element of the New Left that was to be most closely devoted to the critical analysis of society and state.[13] These members of the Frankfurt School, who although deeply conversant with Nietzsche's work mediated it in a manner much different than Foucault did, remained dialecticians in the Hegelian tradition. They relied on Nietzsche's psychological insights while resisting his critique of dialectical thought (though Foucault once acknowledged deep affinities between his work and that of the Frankfurt School, commenting on the noncommunication between French poststructuralism and German critical theory in the post-World War II era).[14] In fact, the Frankfurt School use of Nietzsche was to characterize his more general place in political theory as a semisubterranean influence. More generally, one might say that, with a few important exceptions, in the post-World War II era the role of Nietzsche in political thought was marginal at best and pejorative at worst.[15]

Indeed, one might understand the reintroduction of Nietzsche to the study of politics, especially in the wake of the events of the 1960s, as a symptom of a more profound movement in thought that Foucault helped to nurture. That movement concerned itself with how we are to act in the wake of the cataclysmic events of the World Wars, wars that defined this century as participating in a destructive struggle over politics. For Foucault as well as for many in the Frankfurt School, the very retreat from politics paradoxically is implicated in this politically inspired destruction. In fact, one difficulty in examining Foucault as a philosopher of freedom is that the discussion of freedom as a category of his thought, with certain exceptions, has been obscured because his immediate objects of analysis—oppression, marginality, internment, and the seeming effacement of subjectivity—are all topics that dialectically relate to freedom only as its opposite, or as its lack. And since Foucault eschewed the sort of dialectical critique that enabled a more direct connection of the subject to freedom (through the sort of moves that Adorno and Horkheimer made in *Dialectic of Enlightenment*[16]), he seemed boxed into a corner: a prophet of the death of man, an analyst of the conditions of our confinement, but not a theorist of how we might be free. Of course, one could also claim that Foucault contributed to obscuring the meaning of his work simply because it has been so multifaceted. There have been so many Foucaults from which to choose; the trajectory of Foucault's intellectual career was hardly a smooth one. Which Foucault does one study? There is Foucault the hermeneuticist of suspicion, Foucault the genealogist, Foucault the activist, Foucault the classicist, Foucault the antipsychiatrist, Foucault the anarchist, Foucault the postmodern antihumanist, Foucault the theorist of sexuality, Foucault the serenely stoic classicist . . .

If Foucault secured a certain measure of fame on the American side of the Atlantic as a consequence of the publication of *Discipline and Punish,* his fame was secured with the arrival of the first volume of *The History of Sexuality.* In that later study there seemed to be a crystallization of the themes that emerged in his earlier work concerning power and subjectivity. A shift in emphasis to normalization and biopower, a reconceptualization of the role of the confession, focusing on its quotidian role in the emergence of a sexual subject, and, finally, a treatment of sexuality as a historically embedded set of practices all reasserted and clarified the meaning of Foucault's genealogical project. That project at this point seemed to provide a way to reexamine every aspect of modern truth in light of practices of power. Yet his argument for a nominalism in the study of power and his conclusion concerning the political threshold humanity might be crossing seemed at the same time to operate as a wholesale rejection of modernity. The first volume of *The History of Sexuality* thus confirmed for his critics the idea that Foucault somehow was uninterested in anything other than a wholesale refusal of the conditions of modern life.[17]

Seven years after the appearance of the first volume, two more volumes of *The History of Sexuality* appeared. In them, Foucault engaged in what seemed to be a strong reorientation of his thought toward ancient practices of ethics. Many thought these works, published very shortly before Foucault's death, were a departure from his "political" phase. From this point of view, critics saw Foucault retreating from the strong stances he had taken throughout his intellectual life that were at war with the basic tenets of Enlightenment thought and practice. Alternatively, others believed that in coming to terms with his own mortality Foucault felt somehow liberated, newly free to experiment with alternative practices of self-formation.[18] They saw in his final lectures, which investigated the ancient practice of *parrhesia* (truth telling), confirmation of this departure from his earlier position.

And yet Foucault did not describe his project in such terms, as a departure or break from his thinking about how we are political. In his examination of the practice of parrthesia, he was once again reconfiguring a deep concern with freedom that animated his earlier works, especially those most concerned with the history of our present. The questions of freedom that led him back to the Stoic appropriation of Greek thought, moreover, also reflect his deep concern with the contemporary conditions of our possibilities of being free. Those of us who have been born into or have achieved the status of membership in liberal societies have never been exempt from the concern he expressed regarding the disciplinary character of our freedom. And as the pressures of late modernity challenge the settled forms through which the disciplinary character of freedom is expressed, liberal rights are in danger of becoming anachronistic. This concern becomes clearer in the late work of Foucault. It is a concern to articulate an ethic in response to the failure of our politics to be ethical, a concern for how we might escape the judgment we have imposed upon our selves, a concern for the beauty of being free.

The controversy that attended so much of Foucault's career has given some critics license to call into question his stature as someone who might be able to address important questions of ethics. I think that some of the recent work on Foucault that reduces his thought to his personality operates as a strange confirmation precisely of his ethical edge. The indifference that Foucault expressed regarding the question of who speaks is an ironic and preemptive rebuke to those who have sought to psychologize his work.[19] While many of those who disagree with Foucault have done so for reasons that seem reasonable, too often there has been disagreement in bad faith by some who see Foucault as representing a threat to their hegemony on matters of leftist politics, and by others, who are simply or complicatedly homophobic in their personal politics. Too often, polemicists of the aging New Left have insisted on characterizing Foucault through the lens of his personality, as a writer who deliberately encourages quiescence or who is irresponsible, anarchistic, narcissistic, or even quietist. Their anger at Foucault is, I suspect, a reflection of a peculiar if common irritation:

Foucault is a dangerous destabilizer of their own desires for security. They know too well that such security cannot be attained without taking up the tools of power they once, in their youthful indiscretions, abhorred. And yet the positions they now advocate look too much like the positions they once opposed, as so many of them now seek to influence the governance of others in the most ordinary ways, cozying up to power even as they claim to oppose it. Foucault's insistence on the intimate relationship of power/knowledge makes them uneasy not because he condemns them (such condemnation is for him naive) but because they condemn themselves with their own moralistic claims to speak for others, because they seek to remain as judges, even of their own complicity with the power that shapes them. Indeed, one might claim that the primary focus of Foucault's work as an ethical thinker is intended to enable, or seeks to have the effect of enabling, a rethinking of the paradoxes of the desire for stable identity underlying the claims of these new moralists.[20]

So Foucault's work eventually led him to the suggestion, elliptical but powerful, that the current political way of thinking no longer serves very well most of those who live in this time. That idea in turn implies that the political rationality that informs the interplay between law and order has in our time intensified both a form of sovereign individuality and the legitimacy of totalistic political regimes.[21] But that is not the only insight to which it leads. For Foucault, there is also a radical alterity to our lives that might be revealed through the process of interrogating our political strategies. The condition of radical alterity, at the intersection of what might be termed the infrastructure of power and the superstructure of representation, we might identify as being the zone of our freedom.

This radical alterity of the present is always available to us as a practical alternative to being as we are.[22] This is so not because of the intelligibility of the present but because of its complexity. Indeed, in response to the contemporary condition, Foucault eschewed a simple characterization of the nature of the present:

> [Any diagnosis of the present] does not consist of a simple characterization of what we are but, instead—by following lines of fragility in the present—in managing to grasp why and how that-which-is might no longer be that-which-is. *In this sense, any description must be made in accordance with these kinds*

*of virtual fractures which open up the space of freedom as a space of concrete
freedom, i.e., of possible transformation.* (Emphasis mine)[23]

Transformation is thus not a distant flight away from the conditions of our
being but, instead, a metamorphosis, or morphing, of the virtuality of our
lives, building concretely upon the experience of the present so as to realize
our freedom as a practice.

So I want to suggest at the outset that to understand Foucault sympathetically is not to presume that he presents a rejection of our humanity but,
instead, that he presents a critique of one style of being human that threatens
our continued existence. Put bluntly, our style of being human hides the
very fact that it is a style; it essentializes freedom by de-emphasizing it as
a practice and emphasizing it as a space and thus makes us fail to recognize
the conditions of its construction and destruction, the terms of freedom and
subjection presented to us in the modern age. Resisting this kind of
essentialism requires a certain eclectic attitude, and in this Foucault's work
is exemplary. In a sense, I understand myself to be warranted by Foucault
to construct a Foucault whose concerns fit with the need to think about how
we might be free in terms that will exceed and conflict with those he himself
may have favored. The focus of this volume, then, is on some of his major
works that center on the question of political existence and some of those
works that follow up on his analysis of politics. It is not exhaustive, but
hopefully neither is it without its own rigor.

The Question of Voice

There is yet one final note to make before entering directly into the
themes central to this study. This concerns the issue of what, for lack of
a better term, might be called the question of Foucault's "voice." If
Foucault's interests were extraordinarily widespread, his style of thought
was embodied in a philosophical voice that has disturbed and unsettled most
of those who have listened for its murmur on the written page. Foucault's
voice is alternatively imperious, quiet, violent, gray, anonymous, and
iconoclastic. While it is not my intention to defend or attack that voice in

any of its modes or even to contemplate what it would mean to inhabit its character, I do wish to understand how that voice informs some of the paths of thought traced by it. And even though I wish to explore but one element of it, I also seek to appreciate as many of its tonalities as I can absorb. I understand this vague wish to be important because I think it is connected to whatever efforts we might make to *imagine* some alternatives to the present ways in which we engage in the governance of selves, the ethics of our relationships with each other, and the manner in which we might know how we are free. To engage in an imaginative project of rethinking our selves involves a particular way of understanding some of the connections that might be made between space and the practice of being free and the expressions of their various relationships in aesthetics and ethics. It involves as well a willingness to lose a kind of certainty associated with the solidity of one's own habitation of voice, one's ownership, if you will, of the language through which one enunciates one's self, presenting one's self to the world in the effort to be free. It also entails an element of old-fashioned liberal tolerance, made fresh through an admission of the instabilities of the truths one might admit or reject from serious consideration.

When Foucault meditated on the question of voice in his inaugural lecture at the Collège de France, he made two comments in reference to his own teacher, Jean Hyppolite, one at the beginning and one at the conclusion of his lecture. Each reference reflects the same method of investigation that might apply more generally to anyone who seeks to resume the work he began (a work that was, in turn, a resumption). Foucault said,

> At the moment of speaking, I would have liked to have perceived a nameless voice, long preceding me, leaving me merely to enmesh myself in it, taking up its cadence, and to lodge myself, when no one was looking, in its interstices as if it had paused an instant, in suspense, to beckon me. . . . I know now just what was so awesome about beginning; for it was here, where I speak now, that I listened to that voice, and where its possessor is no longer, to hear me speak.[24]

Although these sentences reflect a complex respect for his predecessor, they also provide advice for anyone who would seek to trace the path of freedom, or one who would follow Foucault's path to understanding how we are free. Proceed as though you have been preceded, lose yourself in the voice of another, and in due course you will realize that you have lost the voice of the one who has gone before and that you have begun to trace a path for yourself. Should you be uncertain as to the depth or authenticity of your own voice, you will have recourse to the memory of your beginning. And should you worry about the stability of that memory, of that voice you now inhabit, Foucault provides you with yet another piece of advice, perhaps his most difficult and ambiguous lesson. In a coda to the conclusion of *The Archaeology of Knowledge,* he writes,

> In each sentence that you pronounce—and very precisely in the one that you are busy writing at this moment, you have been so intent, for so many pages, on answering a question in which you felt yourself personally concerned and who are going to sign this text with your name—in every sentence there reigns the nameless law, the blank indifference: "What does it matter who is speaking; someone has said: what does it matter who is speaking?"[25]

Some of us may well be possessed of a desire to disrupt the reign of blank indifference, even as we accede to the inevitability of its power. In between the enunciation of voice and the inevitable indifference of the nameless law we might wend our way. Yet we may also admit that there is a comfort in the blank indifference that effaces the speaker, an indifference that goes the whole way down. To admit this indifference is to learn a very ancient lesson, but one that is still controversial. It is a lesson we might derive from a reading of *The Book of Job.* Job, when finally confronted with the nameless voice from the whirlwind, responds by saying, "I have heard of you with my ears, but now my eyes have seen you. Therefore I will be quiet, comforted that I am dust."[26] Job's comfort is in his own mortality, but his mortality is also something withheld from him throughout the parable. The withholding of death might be understood as a source of politics, maybe even of what some would call politics proper. Job's comfort comes with the revelation that there is a gap between the moral and the ethical, a contingent quality to nature, a chaos upon which we order things, and upon which our determinations of freedom may be seen. Job's comfort is, I think, also Foucault's. But rather than it leading to a passive stoicism, for Foucault it led to a hyperactivism. After all, for Foucault, if not for Job, regardless of who killed him God is dead.

Focusing on Freedom

I pursue the study of the politics of freedom in Foucault by focusing on the elements that might be said to best characterize the modern understanding of freedom. I want to show how Foucault resists the terms through which freedom is characterized in contemporary discourse, so in Chapter 2 I set in motion an argument concerning the contested meaning of freedom, asking questions about the role of the concept of space as it relates to modern freedom. Using the famous essay by Isaiah Berlin, "Two Concepts of Freedom," as a foil, I attempt to show how the ideas concerning space articulated in some of Foucault's early work operate as a resource for rethinking the debate concerning the meaning of freedom in modern life. I try to demonstrate that Foucault enables a resituating of arguments concerning freedom by concretizing the experiences of agency and situatedness otherwise left abstract by the articulation of freedom in negative and positive terms. By paying attention to freedom's relationship to different constitutions of space I want to enable other arguments concerning the specific character of those categories most associated with its modern articulation—rights, sovereignty, and mobility. In short, the purpose of Chapter 2 is to open an argumentative space about the possibility of freedom as a concrete practice rather than as a situation or condition.

Following upon this argument, throughout Chapter 3 I emphasize a set of related transitions in practices that Foucault identifies as consequential to the emergence of modern politics. Crucially important among these are the migration of sovereignty from king to agent that took place at the end of the medieval period in certain European countries and the reorganization of zones of legality and illegality in those same places. I will suggest that Foucault understands both of these transitions as contributing in a decisive way to the establishment of new, individualized rights in Western countries. They also established a set of prejudices concerning the constitution of spatial relations that enable the simplification of argument entailed in the distinction between negative and positive freedom. This practical establishment of modern rights in turn is coupled to another, distinctly modern development, that of delinquency, a category of personal existence through which the dominant registers of modern life might be negatively signaled and comprehended in relation to each other. The transformation in both the meaning and importance of these organizing categories of personal existence—sovereignty, rights, punishment, individuality, legality, and delinquency—make possible the modern practice of freedom, even as they delimit it.

The purpose of Chapter 3, then, is to outline how Foucault's delineation of these categories within a genealogy of disciplinary society provides a vocabulary for our political way of thinking about freedom. That I try to accomplish this task through a critical reading of *Discipline and Punish* may strike some as an irony of no small dimension, but the key to understanding the place of freedom in the modern age entails understanding the conditions of its internment. Each of these categories, crucial to understanding the shape of freedom's space and condition, is in and of itself worthy of deeper consideration and thought as a political value than can be provided in a short book. As a substitute for, or gesture in the direction of such a discussion, I hope to explain how Foucault's work suggests alternative ways of understanding the emergence and reciprocal influence of these categories. Further, I wish to show how their common emergence is intimately related to the dynamic qualities of disciplinary society and how their further elaboration in our time might provide clues as to new transitions in the conditions of political life that seem to be coming about through a crisis of disciplinary civilization.

The dynamic quality of disciplinary society is too often understated or ignored by critics of *Discipline and Punish*. Instead, most critics pay attention to the extraordinary detail with which disciplinary society operates to ensure that no life goes unmarked. Surveillance is immediately reduced to being a technique in the category of unfreedom. The rigorous organization of time is seen as freezing everyone in place, acting as a form of confinement. But such an approach to the study of disciplinary society misapprehends Foucault's concern with freedom, which is not for him a category or zone in which there is no power/knowledge but is, instead, a style of being in the world that depends on an awareness of how one cares for the world, or, to use George Kateb's phrase, how one has "an attachment to existence."[27] Foucault suggests that if the relationships he describes are as static as is often described by his critics it would mark not a world of power but one of powerlessness. What the operation of power ensures is, in fact, the production of the terms of its contestation. In this light, Foucault's concern with detail is not simply an obsession but is directed toward the acquisition of an intimate knowledge of practices through which people exercise freedom, through which they practice being free.

If we came to know better the style of being free in the modern age, we might also know better what would constitute the crisis of disciplinary society. Because transformative change is possible in "a space of concrete freedom," we can examine the spatial conditions of freedom for signs of its change. From such an examination we might be able to note that disciplinary society and its supporting institutions seem to operate in the second half of this century in what we might call a "state of emergency." This state of emergency, composed of a radically intense exercise of power over bodies, presents a very serious challenge to those of us who hope to see transformations in the conditions of freedom.[28] If our political way of thinking has failed, as seems evidenced by the catastrophes that humankind has experienced in the past century, then how are we to begin to rethink politics? The crisis of discipline in the West signals something, but what? Could it be a harbinger of a new style of freedom, or the prophecy of the worst catastrophe of all, an implosion of power that would result in the destruction of life on an unprecedented scale, or at least a major constriction of freedom?

Some, who point to the rise of totalitarianism in Western societies during this century, suggest that such an implosion may already have occurred, and others have argued that in the wake of the Cold War the primary expressions of this totalitarianism have been overcome. But for Foucault, such arguments are facile at best. There are many ways to approach these questions.[29] I have chosen to focus on what I consider to be a prototypical case of discipline in a state of emergency, or discipline *in extremis,* at its transgressive limit, in order to think about what sort of latencies connect the experience of extreme order with the less thoroughgoing exercise of normalization in our time. For my purposes, the emergence of genocidal concentration camps can be understood as the realization of the "exemplary institutions" of our century. These camps had the annihilation of bodies as their animating spirit. I follow this impulse into the contemporary American carceral by observing certain commonalities in the experience of post-disciplinary internment shared by concentration camp prisoners and prisoners in the modern American prison. For far from being institutions of rehabilitation in a disciplinary sense, these contemporary institutions share certain features with those camps relevant to understanding the future of freedom.

In examining life under the conditions of concentration exemplified by and embodied in these camps and prisons—as discipline that had emanated from the Panopticon—Chapter 4 attempts to trace the decline of discipline and the rise of what might be called new strategies of enclosure by observing certain features of life in the context of life's disallowance. These strategies are described in parts of Foucault's study of the history of sexuality as well as in related writings. They have as their final articulation a new set of exclusions that are potently deathbound. The transformation of disciplinary society into something other than itself depends, as he suggests, on the triumph of a particular kind of relationship of the body to power, the triumph of a particular form of "biopower." Foucault's concern with the history of sexuality is associated with his worry about the possibilities of freedom in a world that had crossed a particular epistemological threshold. At this historical point, the political strategies of nation-states risk much more than had previously been thought possible in order to secure the political arrangements of those who are ruled by them. The phenomenon of mass extermination represents one horrific, if exemplary, form that the disallowance of life has taken and hence needs to be a site from which we might examine a possible experience for many of us, one that remains a dangerous latency in our present. The dramatic intensification and proliferation of the experience of being ghettoized in the great urban centers of the world represents another problem that contains within it threats to the "space of concrete freedom." Nuclear war remains as another such latency, one that I will not explore in this study.[30] Generally, addressing the conditions that allow for the possibility of the disallowance of life on the scales represented by these phenomena requires thinking through the idea of this experience.[31]

There may be objections to the exercise of observation and comparison I undertake in this final chapter by those who adhere to the belief that the lessons of the Holocaust are somehow "beyond" politics. But I think that the claims Foucault advances regarding the intimate relationship of freedom to politics demands a rigorous investigation of that which, by some at least, is seen as an absolute exercise of power beyond the possibility of politics. A more ordinary objection to any attempt to characterize extermination and massive exclusionary movements as the culmination of disciplinary society might be this: Foucault's articulation of power must in the end be totalizing; it must reject the terms of modernity in such a way as to render moot any insight he might have on our existential problems. Hence, if one is to rely upon him, one must participate, at best, in a facile stoicism and, at worst, in a giddy nihilism. Many of Foucault's philosophical critics, especially those who follow Habermas, have implicitly suggested as much by claiming that his approach to the issues of power is "totalizing," leaving no room for negotiation or resistance. On the basis of this argument they suggest that his depiction of disciplinary society allows for no possible response other than implicit or secret appeals to some previously settled "good," such as an implicit Kantian ethics.

While I have already noted how the characterization of Foucault's work as being a total critique of modernity is mistaken, there are other reasons for doubting that he is implicitly dependent on Kant to supply him with an ethical ground on which to stand. First, although Foucault appreciated the way in which Kant provided reasons for engaging in a continual critique of the conditions of modernity, were he to attempt to rely upon the foundations of Kantian ethics he would have grounded his work in arguments concerning the formal reasons for an adherence to such constructs as the categorical imperative. But he resisted such thinking; it was not his "style" in the most expansive sense of that term. One might note that, as the French translator of Kant's *Anthropology,* Foucault appreciated Kant's critical edge too much to do other than resist the Kantian impulse to command. Alternatively, if one attends to the notion that Foucault was a thinker who was deeply practical—his work calls attention to practices, their histories, their plural geneses, their lumpy transformations—then one might see how his concern with practices helped shape his political thought. From the study of practices comes an awareness of their persistent and tenacious character, to be sure, but also their contingency and mutability.

I attempt to think about extermination in this context because, among other things, the creation of the death camps was the result of a set of practical innovations designed to disallow life rather than more simply to execute enemies of sovereign power. In that, they have something important in common with the modern prison, which exists on the same plane. The practical element of the camps perhaps intensifies the need to think about them with care, with a caution that would prevent one from mistakenly suggesting that the practices that occurred in them were so common as to be a ubiquitous possibility for all of us. On the other hand, one would not wish to look away from the window that Auschwitz opens.[32] This practice of the Nazis engendered resistances and responses. Those responses might move us toward a sort of political ethics less encumbered by the rigidities of the sort of categorical distinctions that have so deeply been implicated in our catastrophes. For me the most important response to the possibility of extermination is enunciated with care and subterfuge by the person I consider to be the exemplary writer of this experience, Primo Levi. For Levi, I hope to argue, the experience of seduction marks the most important, if also most painful, response to the deathboundness of Auschwitz and hence signals a transformative moment in the concrete space of freedom.

Foucault was never clearer about the possibilities of practical transformation than in his work on ethics that followed his critique of our practices of politics. I turn explicitly to the problem of ethics in my conclusion. There I try to understand what is at stake in the widespread perception of the supposed distance Foucault achieves from the concerns of the present. I try not to extend the ancient idea of care of self to the present but to show how elements of the present are necessarily informed by the technologies of the self rooted in that distant past. The mediations of time that must be negotiated in order to make use of the insights that Foucault sketched in these last books constitute my own point of departure from Foucault and the conclusion of this book.[33]

* * *

All books are written with audiences in mind. I have written this one as an occasion to share a particular set of concerns regarding the possibilities of our age, to enter a discussion with anyone who is concerned about the proliferation of the normalizing judgments of our day and those who seek to aim at the heart of the present in thinking through, to whatever ends they must, the logics of the practices of our time. Such an audience will be worried, too, about judgments concerning the quality of responsible work. My own worries about such judgments are parochial. I get most nervous when the voice of responsibility emanates from fellow scholars who, instead of aiming at the heart of the present, demonstrably aim only to re-create a sense of middle to ensure the reenforcement of an imagined consensus, which (always and only) retrospectively turns out to be merely another norm. Such fellow travelers of the normal have raised in me deep suspicions because the force of their work, so often against their explicit intentions, has been diffusely supportive of the most reactionary politicians who seek to rule our desires. But they are not the only people complicit with the powers that be these days. All of us lend our support to those powers every time we remain silent in the face of our governors' perfidies. I worry not only because such silence might damage the possibility of freeing space but also because I worry about my own commitments and betrayals. It is a subject worthy of worry, I think.

In a late interview, Foucault outlined two forms of criticism and endorsed but one. After questioning the value of the kind of critical judgment that condemns, a criticism that seeks to identify responsible parties, he wrote,

> I can't help but dream about a kind of criticism that would not try to judge, but to bring an ouvre, a book, a sentence, an idea to life; it would light fires, watch the grass grow, listen to the wind, and catch the sea-foam in the breeze and scatter it. It would multiply, not judgments, but signs of existence. . . . Criticism that hands down sentences puts me to sleep; I'd like a criticism of scintillating leaps of imagination. It would not be sovereign or dressed in red. It would bear the lightning of possible storms.[34]

If the politics of our present were only to be judged and condemned rather than investigated for the signs of existence that may be contained within them, for the inventions that might be enabled by them, and for the creative leaps that might be lying dormant in the minds of us who live in the space of late disciplinary society we would not need to think with Foucault. Ironically, though, the judgments of the present incited him and may have (perversely) inspired him to make his most audacious claims, including the desire to be anonymous. Were his wish fulfilled, to the relief of many of us and perhaps to the posthumous relief of Foucault himself, he might disappear without a trace. For Foucault's work leads elsewhere, not to the completion of a project but to the possibility of thinking in a different way, discovering how we are free other-wise. To create a better understanding of our political way of thinking, we need to release ourselves from the modes of judgment that would consign us to a place behind a table, judging, once again, by condemning.

Between the play of the institutions that have produced us—institutions that we continue to reproduce even as we resist their effects—and the fearful emptiness that contemplating their loss evokes in us, Foucault identifies how we may be free beings. He refers us not to a space unfettered or alone but to a busy intersection. It is marked with many lines to be crossed or erased, so many as to have created many shades of gray. This indeterminate site establishes many themes to be challenged and many truths to be found and lost. To inhabit such a space, perhaps that is the impossible task that has been given to us as political beings. Yet, with Foucault we might begin to understand that the paradox of the human condition is that we engage in such impossible endeavors all of the time.

Notes

1. See "The Political Technology of Individuals," in Luther Martin et al., eds., *Technologies of the Self: A Seminar with Michel Foucault* (Amherst: University of Massachusetts Press, 1988), 161.

2. Jürgen Habermas, "Taking Aim at the Heart of the Present," *University Publishing* (September 1984): 1.

3. Michel Foucault, *The History of Sexuality, Volume 1. An Introduction,* trans. Robert Hurley (New York: Pantheon, 1978), 143. The phrase "the fate of the political" is also the subtitle of Dana Villa's book *Arendt and Heidegger* (Princeton University Press, 1996), an important study of the influence of Martin Heidegger on the political thought of Hannah Arendt and, in turn, on how Arendt conceived of the possibilities of political action in the modern age. Heidegger's influence on Foucault is immense and crucial to understanding his work, but the Heideggerian influence on Foucault is mediated by Foucault's understanding of Nietzsche. For Foucault's comments on Heidegger's influence, see "Final Interview: Michel Foucault," in *Raritan* V (Summer 1985): 8-9. In that interview, Foucault suggests that Heidegger and Nietzsche are the most important philosophers for him. He suggests something else as well, which has served as a caution to me as I have tried to write this book (a book that would, in a perfect world, lie unread and unnoticed should I choose to continue to use Foucault as an instrument for my own thought). He says, "I think it is important to have a small number of authors with whom one thinks, with whom one works, but about whom one does not write" (p. 9).

The question of Arendt's relationship to Foucault, as providing a possible alternative conceptualization of freedom, is touched upon by Villa on page 206 of his *Arendt and Heidegger.*

4. For a series of excursions into the politics of personal identity and its operation of exclusion that have had a powerful influence on my understanding of Foucault, see William

E. Connolly, *Identity\Difference: Democratic Negotiations of Political Paradox* (Ithaca, NY: Cornell University Press, 1991).

5. I do not know how to weigh the costs of liberalism. But I also think that no one else does, despite the extraordinary amount of effort that has been made to determine that cost. The history of Marxism can itself be seen as a response to the desire to determine the cost of liberalism. But in the wake of Marx we must still ask, is liberalism the ancillary ideology of capitalism, or is it a semiautonomous realm of life that is itself a primary source of its own good and evil? How does one think about the costs of the economic organization of life without engaging in the very struggle to end politics that determines the danger that is Foucault's concern? Despite the lack of an answer, and perhaps the ultimate undecidability of this question, it must remain a question for as long as liberalism is the predominant shape that freedom takes.

6. Two contemporary liberal thinkers who fit this description are Richard Flathman and George Kateb. See the former's *Willful Liberalism: Voluntarism and Individuality in Political Theory and Practice* (Ithaca, NY: Cornell University Press, 1992) and the latter's *The Inner Ocean: Individualism and Democratic Culture* (Ithaca, NY: Cornell University Press, 1992), each of which confronts and absorbs Foucaultian themes in implicit and explicit ways.

7. Whether framed in terms of Jürgen Habermas's communicative ethics or Ernesto Laclau's and Chantal Mouffe's call for radical democracy, contemporary post-Marxist formulations of "what is to be done" are largely silent on issues of state power, or at best vaguely reformist. See Habermas, *The Theory of Communicative Action* (2 vols.), trans. Thomas McCarthy (Boston: Beacon, 1984, 1987).

8. The power of their critique of freedom is currently being tested in the realm of practical politics in the United States especially, where the policies encouraged by the fundamentalist right are currently, however imperfectly, being implemented.

9. See William E. Connolly, *Political Theory and Modernity* (New York: Basil Blackwell, 1988), 189.

10. For a study of this history, see David Ricci, *Community Power and Democratic Theory: The Logic of Political Analysis* (New York: Random House, 1971). For a powerful and incisive analysis of the reasons for the emergence of behavioralism in the post-World War II era in the United States, see Frederick Dolan, *Allegories of America: Narratives, Metaphysics, Politics* (Ithaca, NY: Cornell University Press, 1994), esp. chap. 3, "Cold War Metaphysics."

11. For two recent studies that emphasize this dimension of Foucault's work in the context of gay identity, see Leo Bersani, *Homos* (Cambridge, MA: Harvard University Press, 1995), and David Halperin, *Saint Foucault: Toward a Gay Hagiography* (New York: Oxford University Press, 1995).

12. See especially Allan Bloom, *The Closing of the American Mind* (New York: Simon & Schuster, 1987), and Dinesh DeSousa, *Illiberal Education* (New York: Free Press, 1991).

13. For an overview of the history of the Frankfurt School, see Martin Jay, *The Dialectical Imagination* (Boston: Little, Brown, 1973). There is as yet no systematic intellectual history of the integration of critical theory into the American academy, although the book that comes closest, while marred by a deeply polemic and resentful posture, is Russell Jacoby's *The Last Intellectuals: American Culture in the Age of Academe* (New York: Basic Books, 1987). There also exists a variety of right-wing polemics against the academic left, which are basically of no value other than as symptoms of anti-intellectualism.

14. See Foucault, "How Much Does It Cost for Reason to Tell the Truth?" in *Foucault Live*, ed. Sylvère Lotringer (New York: Semiotext(e), 1988), 241-2.

15. For instance, the influential Leo Strauss and his students publicly presented Nietzsche as a nihilist. See Werner Dannhauser, "Friedrich Nietzsche," in Leo Strauss and Joseph Cropsey, eds., *The History of Political Thought* (Chicago: Rand McNally, 1963). It seems as though they also had deep affinities for Nietzsche that they kept secret. See Shadia Drury, *The Political Ideas of Leo Strauss* (New York: St. Martin's, 1990). For an excellent overview of approaches to the study of Nietzsche, see Mark Warren, *Nietzsche and Political Philosophy* (Cambridge: MIT Press, 1988), especially pp. 1-12. An important exception to the neglect of Nietzsche as a source for political theory during this era is the work of Hannah Arendt.

16. Max Horkheimer and Theodor Adorno, *Dialectic of Enlightenment* (New York: Seabury Press, 1969), e.g., 226.

17. This seemed especially true of Jürgen Habermas. See his *The Philosophical Discourse of Modernity* (Cambridge: MIT Press, 1987).

18. This is one of the ways in which James Miller attempts to narrate Foucault's life in his self-described "sensationalist" biography of Foucault. See Miller, *The Passion of Michel Foucault* (New York: Simon & Schuster, 1993).

19. See Miller, *The Passion of Michel Foucault*, for the primary example of this genre.

20. Perhaps the political theorist who has done the most to explicate the political ethics in Foucault's work is William Connolly. See especially his *The Augustinian Imperative: A Reflection on the Politics of Morality* (Newbury Park, CA: Sage, 1993).

21. Foucault, "The Political Technology of Individuals," 162.

22. One other thinker who is evocative of Foucault on this matter is Walter Benjamin. See especially his "Theses on the Philosophy of History," in *Illuminations*, ed. Hannah Arendt, trans. Harry Zohn (New York: Schocken, 1969).

23. See "Critical Theory/Intellectual History," in Lawrence D. Kritzman, ed., *Michel Foucault: Philosophy, Politics, Culture* (New York: Routledge, 1988), 36.

24. See "The Discourse on Language," a translation by Rupert Swyer of Foucault's Inaugural Lecture found as an appendix to *The Archaeology of Knowledge* (New York: Harper & Row, 1976), 215, 237.

25. See "Politics and the Study of Discourse," in Graham Burchell et al., eds., *The Foucault Effect: Studies in Governmentality* (Chicago: University of Chicago Press, 1991), 72.

26. *The Book of Job,* translated and with an introduction by Stephen Mitchell (San Francisco: North Point Press, 1987), 88. For a gloss on Job sensitive to its Foucaultian moments, see Connolly, *The Augustinian Imperative*, chap. 1, "Voices from the Whirlwind."

27. See George Kateb, "Thinking about Human Extinction (II): Nietzsche and Heidegger," in *The Inner Ocean.*

28. The idea of a state of emergency in this context is one that I think is first developed by Walter Benjamin. See his essay, "Surrealism: The Last Snapshot of the European Intelligentsia," in *Reflections*, ed. Peter Demetz, trans. Edmund Jephcott (New York: Harcourt Brace Jovanovich, 1978). Benjamin also mentions the "state of emergency" in his "Theses on the Philosophy of History," in *Illuminations*, ed. Hannah Arendt. More recently, this idea has been developed by Paul Virilio. See "Part Four: The State of Emergency," in his *Speed and Politics*, trans. Mark Polizotti (New York: Semiotext(e), 1986). See also Michael Taussig, *The Nervous System* (New York: Routledge, 1992).

29. Two recent collections of essays are very helpful in tracing alternative paths of exploration of what, for lack of a better term, one might call postdisciplinary society. See the collection of essays gathered in the wake of a conference on Foucault's work (organized by the Michel Foucault Center, Francois Ewald, Director). See *Michel Foucault, Philosopher,*

trans. Timothy Armstrong (New York: Routledge, 1992). Also see Burchell et al., eds., *The Foucault Effect.*

30. Instead, I refer readers to two books that attempt to study this matter in light of (different) understandings of Foucault and of other poststructuralist thinkers: Kateb, *The Inner Ocean,* and William Chaloupka, *Knowing Nukes: The Politics and Culture of the Atom* (Minneapolis: University of Minnesota Press, 1992).

31. I will focus primarily on some of the works of Primo Levi to illuminate this difficult path, especially his first memoir of life in Auschwitz. See Primo Levi, *Survival at Auschwitz: The Nazi Assault on Humanity,* trans. Stuart Woolf (New York: Collier, 1959).

32. I repeat here a metaphor developed in Zygmunt Bauman's *Modernity and the Holocaust* (Ithaca, NY: Cornell University Press, 1989), viii.

33. It bears repeating that my study of Foucault's approach to ethics is deeply informed by conversations with William Connolly. See especially the final chapter of his *The Augustinian Imperative.* I have also found John Rajchman, *Truth and Eros: Foucault, Lacan and the Question of Ethics* (New York: Routledge, 1991), to be of great help in situating Foucault's work within the context of French structuralism. Finally, a study of the relationship of poststructuralism and anarchy by Todd May, *The Political Philosophy of Poststructuralist Anarchism* (University Park: Pennsylvania State University Press, 1994), resonates strongly with the political perspective I have become sensitive to in Foucault, whether one labels it anarchism or not.

34. See "The Masked Philosopher," in Kritzman, ed., *Michel Foucault: Philosophy, Politics, Culture,* 326.

2

Freedom and Space

In civilizations without boats, dreams dry up, espionage takes the place of
adventure, and the police take the place of pirates.

—"Of Other Spaces"

During the Persian Gulf War of 1990-91 the world witnessed for the
first time the deployment of a technology known as the Navstar
Global Positioning System (GPS). Developed by the American Department of Defense to keep troops informed of their location, the GPS
is composed of a series of satellites in a fixed orbit, each of which transmits
a signal to earth receivers. Anyone who has access to the system is able
to learn his or her position on the face of the planet (and potentially the
position of others) with extraordinary precision. As a result of this new

---

Epigraph taken from a lecture by Michel Foucault, "Of Other Spaces," trans. Jay Misowiez,
diacritics, Spring 1986, 27.

technology, maps themselves now can become as indefinitely precise as the one represented in the allegory of the Chinese Emperor's map. Troops in the desert, motorists in Tokyo traffic, geologists in the Yukon, pedestrians in New York City, commuters in Southern California—all might avail themselves of the signals transmitted from these satellites (or might not, depending upon access to the signal, which due to security fears is sometimes scrambled in regions of the world, such as central Canada, that are sensitive to the pathways of nuclear warhead delivery systems). The GPS seems to be the definitive solution to what one enthusiast characterizes as perhaps the oldest problem facing mankind, establishing with precision "where he was and where he was going."[1]

But the puzzle of location is never solved by mapping alone. In an installation in New York City in 1994 that investigated the limits and promise of GPS technology, architect Laura Kurgan has provided a compelling demonstration of the (always) incomplete character of precise location. Kurgan attends to the strange consequences that have followed the knowledge of precise location afforded by access to the GPS, making it the linchpin of her exhibit.[2] Kurgan's idea is to turn the building that houses the installation (the Storefront for Art and Architecture) into a GPS receiver and then to plot the location of the building site through satellite triangulation. In the act of showing the observer how the GPS works, she demonstrates that the connection between satellites and receiver creates an immense imaginary canopy, a vast space composed of the lines of information through which location is plotted. The installation itself becomes a trace, the representational residue of a new cyberspace, connecting a site on the ground to several sites in outer space.[3]

Within this surveyed immensity, position on a site is realized as an abstract location, a point on a matrix, neutral in the sense of lacking any content. Within the strategies of GPS positioning, the more precise the location, the more absolutely devoid of space the site itself becomes, until the point substitutes for site itself. But the closer one comes to this ideal termination point, the closer one comes as well to realizing that there is a series of paradoxes entailed in the realization of complete location.

The primary paradox unveiled by the GPS is this: To be precisely located on a map is a new way of being lost. Once it is plotted with precision on a grid, location at a site is displaced by representation in cyberspace. This abstraction of space has profound consequences at the level of experience. When one loses one's sense of place, a sense that seemingly always has been associated with being at a site, the disorientation one experiences is not that of being lost but of losing the ability to know whether one is lost or found. Another way of describing this phenomenon is to suggest the effacement of spatial distinctions: one loses the situational places that exist inside the spatial constructs that enable one to know whether one is lost or found. But simultaneous with that loss comes the possibility of something new—the creation of an ambiguous space within which it is possible to imagine more than one object sharing the same place. Lost and found, previously opposing if complementary experiences, collapse into each other in the context of a decontextualization that emerges as the most common situation—the common denominator—of life in this era. Such a blurring of the conditions of being lost and found is evidenced by the fact that traditional geographical considerations are beginning to fade in political importance, displaced in the realm of modern conflict by the informational needs of the strategic itself, affectively (that is, reactively) expressed in that realm through the representational imperatives of strong claims to national and ethnic identity.[4]

One might think of the GPS as a representative technology that expresses relatively recent common sense, what might be called the common sense of the late modern. This recent common sense was noted with astonishment almost forty years ago by Hannah Arendt, who begins *The Human Condition* with a statement asserting the unprecedented importance of the 1957 launching of the Sputnik satellite.[5] For Arendt, the technical accomplishment of departing from earth is perhaps most surprising for how it has been received by so many of the peoples of the world as a sign of the hope that humankind might someday follow these satellites and leave its earthly prison. Arendt argues that this inchoately expressed desire to leave the earth is a sign of the incapacity of modern men and women to act in the world, to find a way to express themselves in terms compatible with the prerequisites of worldliness. For her, the capacity to imagine the world as a place of action, to understand, in fact, that the world is more than the merely earthly, is intimately connected to the ability of humans to comprehend the meaning of freedom and thus to be free. She seems convinced that the capacity for action has diminished in modern times because the possibility of new beginnings is threatened by overwhelming the human condition by technology.

In a limited sense, Arendt might be understood as an early postmodernist, making a major theme of her work the particular exhaustion of the resources of modernity to address the problems its very success has created, although many of her contemporary interpreters would resist such a claim.[6] More generally, it might be said that with the advent of postmodernity, the predominant techniques by which freedom is situated seem to have become more visible, even as freedom itself has become less fungible. This visibility is either signaled by or is the result of the recent appearance of devices such as the GPS, devices that make explicit the often obscure arguments of philosophers of freedom by showing how their arguments rest upon implicit conceptualizations of space. Thus we might note that the GPS may be as important for its enactment of the theoretical connection between arcane information and its popular dissemination as for the practical task of world battlefield surveillance for which it was designed. Such an observation would also be consistent with Arendt, who was able to note that the emergence of a feeling that the world itself is a prison first came to expression in popular cultural reactions to a war technology, not in the thought of philosophers.

In a similar way, the relationship of freedom to space is brought to common attention through the emergence of televisual and computer technologies that have culminated in the creation of cyberspace, which is itself another popular formation, a product of the technological realm's focus on delineation of realms of space. In short, it is now difficult to doubt that questions of space—questions concerning its constitution and its role in the understandings of freedom developed by those who inhabit it—now must inevitably inform any serious contemporary discussion of the meaning of freedom.[7]

Although there has been an extraordinary renaissance in the study of space in recent years, this realm of scholarship has not seemed to have much of an impact on the most dominantly theorized discussions of freedom, that is, those of contemporary liberal political theory. For the most part, space is assumed in liberal theory to be a neutral field which may be divided into public and private. Perhaps the closest that one might come to a discussion that challenges these boundary conditions is in the realm of modern commercial law, specifically the field of intellectual property rights, with its sensitivity to the incursions of technology into arguments about the violability of the property of personality, and which takes as its subject how the blurring of boundaries has an impact on the realm of liberal privacy.[8] However, the role of space as an element in being free implicitly serves as the dominant means through which all assessments of the extent and quality of freedom are made. To investigate questions of space in relationship to freedom thus seems to require a reassessment of the dominant set of assumptions concerning how space implicitly informs most contemporary formulations of freedom. I take the liberal tradition, in its complex and messy genealogy, to be that tradition that has contributed the most to giving shape to those dominant formulations. So, in a sense, I wish to engage here in an exercise of retrieval, a reconstruction of some of the spatial premises upon which liberal freedom is developed.[9]

Such a reconstruction does not leave liberalism unaltered. Indeed, by thinking through Sir Isaiah Berlin's study of the two concepts of freedom in light of Foucault's early formulations concerning space, I hope to highlight two elements of Foucault's thought that may be consequential to the future study of freedom and that may operate to revitalize liberal theory.[10] First, I examine Foucault's idea of the heterotopia, a complex spatial assemblage that vastly complicates the abstract formulas of spaces that predominate in Berlin's discussions of negative and positive freedom.[11] Second, I examine the relative absence of a sense of agency in Foucault's initial formulations concerning space, a silence concerning what for liberals is perhaps the most important question concerning freedom. I will suggest that this silence is not a deficiency but is, instead, a strategic move that enables him to reconstruct the thought of freedom in his later analysis of disciplinary society, on the one hand, and the normalization of sexuality, on the other. Foucault's thought is more continuous in this sense than many critics have acknowledged.[12] Foucault's silence concerning freedom in these earlier essays and monographs is not born of an imputed structuralist hostility to the idea of freedom itself but, instead, of a very important insight: that the realization of freedom through the medium of agency is itself a *dangerous* enterprise, an enterprise that is liminal in important and fragile ways.[13] It is important to emphasize this fragility because an emphasis on an agency that is clear and somehow unproblematic obscures the powers that establish the grounds upon which agents are determined as free.[14] For Foucault, a reconstitution of the conditions that determine how we might come to know freedom serves as a preface to his later encounter with the dangers associated with freedom's expression in modern experience. His attempt to work through those dangers, to problematize them, is rooted in his understanding of space. He wants to show how their constructions establish the terms through which there might be the expression of new rights that are not as closely dependent upon dangerous relationships as they currently are conceived as being.

If we are to understand how Foucault thinks of freedom, we also must comprehend how he anticipates the range of contests over the habitations and exercises of the seemingly abstract spaces of liberal freedom. These are the habitations that are given their contemporary empirical realization as much in the indefinite cyberspaces created by techniques, such as are deployed through the GPS, as they are in the most architecturally advanced spaces of surveillance, traditionally understood. But that is not all. Beneath the reordering of the meaning of space that informs Foucault's project is a large and enduring question concerning the metaphysical foundations of the modern age. He proceeds from a still underestimated Nietzschean insight, that the death of God has the most profound historical consequences. As Foucault once wrote, in suitably controversial terms,

> Discourse is not life: its time is not your time; in it, you will not be reconciled to death; you may have killed God beneath the weight of all that you have said; but don't imagine that, with all that you are saying, you will make a man that will live longer than you.[15]

These days, given the resurgence of belief in God in its most virulently fundamentalist form, one might ask whether people have been more irritated at his expression of agreement with Nietzsche in his pronouncement concerning the death of God than in his claim concerning the eventual erasure of man. But Foucault's seemingly harsh prediction concerning the fate of man—one he makes, by the way, for himself as well as us—is designed neither to celebrate nor to mourn the coming to pass of this circumstance. Instead, Foucault wants to encourage us to allow ourselves to know better what we must work through if we are to come to terms with the conditions of life as we have established it and the representations that have given rise to our political orders.

Other Spaces

There are several occasions in his early work when Foucault discusses space and its relationship to freedom, even if he does so in ways that are not readily or directly assimilable to the more explicit analysis of visibility and power that he pursued in his later work. An early example of his concern with the overlapping of space and power is found in the analyses that comprise *The Order of Things.* The purpose of that study, he writes in the preface, is to uncover the deepest strata of meaning that composes Western culture. The very idea of archaeology suggests that there are levels to the organization of space that correspond to particular ways in which knowledge comes into being in different eras.

From the limit-experience of the Other to the constituent forms of medical knowledge, and from the latter to the order of things and the conceptions of the Same, what is available to archaeological analysis is the whole of Classical knowledge, or rather, the threshold that separates us from Classical thought and constitutes our modernity. It was upon this threshold that the strange figure of knowledge called man first appeared and revealed a space proper to the human sciences. In attempting to uncover the deepest strata of Western culture, I am restoring to our silent and apparently immobile soil its rifts, its instability, its flaws; and it is the same ground that is once more stirring under our feet.[16]

The ground stirring beneath our feet is to be the site of hope for Foucault in his later writings. In this early formulation the question of the fate of man is noted, famously, in the conclusion of *The Order of Things*—"As the archaeology of our thought easily shows, man is an invention of recent date. And one that is perhaps nearing its end."[17] This fateful prediction has been read apocalyptically by many. But one might see this phrase as reflective of a persistent theme in Foucault's work: he seeks to show us how we are not as we seem to be, how we are not simply the sum of our representations, even our most profound ones, such as "man." In this early work he mixes metaphors: the aural and the visual combine and disturb our ground. The mixing of metaphors has as its purpose the exposure of a space that might make a noise and would no longer be silent in its immobility. We might imagine this noise as the noise of freedom.

Foucault begins *The Order of Things* with a discussion of Velàzquez's masterpiece, *Las Meninas.* His beginning, as is often the case in his books, is intended to resonate with the themes developed in subsequent essays, in this case, to present a strong enactment of the epistemological break that for Foucault heralds the beginning of the modern era. By describing a shift in strategies of representation enacted by Velàzquez, Foucault hopes to prepare his readers to accept his more general thesis concerning the new order of representation that unfolded during what he calls "the Classical Age." The core of this shift is the establishment of an epistemological position from which we might imagine the possibility of there being a pure representation. Foucault argues that the implication of the viewer into the field of knowledge that might be gained from viewing the painting is accomplished by Velàzquez's set of visual gestures, all of which refer the viewer to a position exterior to the picture itself. Velàzquez accomplishes this by establishing lines of composition that are only completed through an explicit acknowledgment by the viewer of the very doubleness the painting is attempting to represent. He represents a mirror, and in that mirror the sovereign couple gazes into the field of the painting itself and can be seen to see themselves. Foucault writes, "That space where the king and his wife hold sway belongs equally well to the artist and to the spectator: in the depths of the mirror there could also appear—there ought to appear— the anonymous face of the passerby and that of Velàzquez."[18] Implied here may be a suggestion of a particular democratic wish, a leveling of the field of knowledge, a mutability of sovereignty, even the sovereignty of the gaze. This suggestion, again barely present here, emerges more explicitly in his later work.

In *The Order of Things,* the question of space is also already a question of power. Foucault presents two major arguments during this period that anticipate his more explicit study of power in his later work. These are contained in two essays that can serve as responses to and summaries of his positions concerning the relationship of language to representation and space to imagination. From these essays we might see how Foucault comes to address, in *Discipline and Punish* and the works that surround it, the conflict between sovereignty (which is the bearer of the positive liberty of modern states) and rights (which signify the negative liberty borne by individuals).

The first of these essays is actually a lecture but is hardly an occasional piece, having much more the feel of a summary and transition. In March 1967, Foucault gave a lecture on the question of space. The lecture presents a simple thesis. Foucault suggests that if the nineteenth century had as its great obsession the question of history "our epoch will perhaps above all be the epoch of space."[19] He claims, summarizing the very recently intellectual history of which he was perceived to be a part, that the very idea of structuralism has been a response to this epochal demand concerning the primacy of space. Structuralism, in this sense, is a moment that recognizes the historical emergence of a new understanding of space (but one that is itself destined to be eclipsed once that moment is realized by itself, and in that sense, it is fatally determined in its intellectual trajectory).[20] Foucault goes on to identify three moments in the history of space since the medieval period of European history. The Middle Ages, he suggests, was a space of emplacement, in which there was a clear demarcation between order and disorder. "There were places where things had been put because they had been violently displaced, and then on the contrary places where things found their natural ground and stability." Foucault contrasted this space to that opened up by Galileo.

> For the real scandal of Galileo's work lay not so much in his discovery, or rediscovery, that the earth revolved around the sun, but in his constitution of an infinite, and infinitely open, space. In such a space the place of the Middle Ages turned out to be dissolved, as it were; a thing's place was no longer anything but a point in its movement, just as the stability of a thing was only its movement indefinitely slowed down. In other words, starting with Galileo and the seventeenth century, extension was substituted for localization.[21]

Extension later is itself substituted for by the site, the contemporary technique for distributing space. "The site is defined by relations of proximity between points or elements; formally, we can describe these relations as series, trees, or grids."[22] Although Foucault is readily able to distinguish these kinds of spaces, he also suggests that the very identification of the techniques through which space was distributed was itself a process that had not advanced very far historically. He writes as though space, unlike time, had not been "desanctified" in practice, even if such a desanctification had occurred in theory. Foucault's citation of the scandal of Galileo is quite apt in this regard. The political impact of his assertion concerning the openness of space unsettles the foundations not only of the medieval place but of the religious political order that depends upon a closed, definite site of existence for its ability to govern truth. Galileo's insight on space thus was profoundly political. As Bertolt Brecht notes (with typical Brechtian irony) in his play *Life of Galileo*, "And the earth tools gaily around the sun, and the fishwives, merchants, princes, cardinals and even the Pope roll around with it. The universe lost its center overnight."[23] Although Galileo was forced by the Vatican to recant his views, the desanctification of the sacred space of the Middle Ages nevertheless unfolded.[24]

If the cosmology of the Middle Ages was shattered by Galileo's revision of space, the successive attempts to stabilize the meaning of space have played a subterranean role in the history of political thought ever since. In his 1967 lecture, Foucault directly addresses the most important issues that flow from the desanctification of space (issues that liberals have been most deeply concerned *not to address*). He writes,

> Perhaps our life is still governed by a certain number of oppositions that remain inviolable, that our institutions and practices have not yet dared to break down. These are oppositions that we regard as simple givens: for example between public space and private space, between family space and social space, between cultural space and useful space, between the space of leisure and that of work. All these are still nurtured by the hidden presence of the sacred.[25]

The desanctification of space is a task that ultimately forces us to face the death of God, for there can be no inviolability that does not invoke some greater sovereignty. But it is no easy matter to address the consequences of the death of God, and, as Foucault demonstrates in other places (following Nietzsche), taking seriously those consequences explodes the metaphorical foundations upon which the modern constitution of space is based.

This argument is profoundly disturbing for those who would attempt to displace questions concerning space away from the discussion of freedom. (And here I hope to adumbrate the argument that Foucault might make against a liberal such as Isaiah Berlin.) Foucault begins by arguing quite simply that the conditions of space as we live it have not yet been adequately investigated in the contemporary era. Those spaces that fail to exhibit a certain openness, a certain ability to allow for contradictory juxtapositioning, will fail as well to provide a renewal of imagination without which no sense of freedom can thrive. In other words, the conditions of freedom themselves are spatial. Foucault insists, however, that "we do not live in a homogeneous and empty space, but on the contrary in a space thoroughly imbued with quantities and perhaps thoroughly fantasmatic as well."[26]

Foucault identifies two kinds of spaces where juxtaposition and contradiction are intensely experienced: utopias, spaces of pure imagination that present societies with perfectly ideal versions of their governing principles; and heterotopias, which concern Foucault much more, as they are, in his words, "real sites."[27] Heterotopias correspond with, or more precisely, respond to, the generally heterogeneous character of external space that produces the common understandings and communicative links through which life proceeds. Heterotopias are scenes in which elements of existence otherwise unconnected to each other connect. He suggests that they are "something like counter-sites, a kind of effectively enacted utopia in which the real sites, the other real sites that can be found within a culture, are simultaneously represented, contested, and inverted."[28]

Foucault sets out to describe the extent and limits of heterotopias, their relationship to more ordinary spaces of life, and their role in relationship to freedom. In his sketch he suggests that heterotopias are governed by six general principles. First, heterotopias are socially ubiquitous, which means that they are a constant of every social group. Although no universal categorization of them can be made, they generally have been of two types, what he calls "heterotopias of crisis" and "heterotopias of deviance." Crisis heterotopias are privileged or sacred spaces, places where forbidden rites occur. They are associated with rites of passage and other moments of transition from one state of being to another. Honeymoon trips and boarding schools are the two examples he provides (examples closely associated with transitions in the sexual status of those who enter into them). Others might be Amer-Indian vision quests or any sites where moments of change in the status of a person are marked. Foucault suggests that such heterotopias have become rarer in our time, "being replaced by what we might call heterotopias of deviance."[29] Rest homes, psychiatric hospitals, prisons, and retirement homes are places apart from the rest of society designed to segregate those whose behavior deviates from a required norm or mean. This shift from the heterotopia of crisis to that of deviance is historically consonant with Foucault's tracing of the confinement of madness and the birth of clinical medicine in his earliest work.

The second principle that Foucault enunciates "is that a society, as its history unfolds, can make an existing heterotopia function in a different fashion; for each heterotopia has a precise and determined function within a society, and the same heterotopia can, according to the synchrony of the culture in which it occurs, have one function or another."[30] He presents as his example what he calls the "strange heterotopia of the cemetery." Cemeteries once were centrally located in towns and cities. Their function was then, as now, to hold the remains of bodies. But just about every element of that function has undergone a transformation of meaning through a transformation of emphasis. When a strong belief in the resurrection of bodies held sway, concern over the status of specific bodies was minimal. Hence, the charnel houses and the commingling of bodies as they decayed was of little concern to the members of medical communities of belief. But with the decline of such belief, death became individualized, everyone came to have "his or her own little box in which to decay"; and death itself became associated with illness, so that a segregation of the dead became logical, and cemeteries moved to the suburbs and countryside.[31] In short, the connections made through a heterotopia are not determined by the heterotopia itself but by the contents a heterotopia's placement brings into play. Its position is crucial to the experiences that people will have, the ways in which they will understand themselves and the importance (or lack of importance) of what they do. But a heterotopia, by its form and function (and this is Foucault's third principle concerning their formation), is a place where it is possible for incompatible sites to be brought together. This function depends upon a necessary openness to the cross-connections such bringing together provides: chronologically and spatially, such an openness has varied greatly.

The fourth principle associated with the heterotopia has to do with its particular relationship to time: it usually intensifies certain chronological effects, by either serving as a repository for what might be called the products of time (museums and libraries, for instance) or as depositories of time itself (as in festivals, fairs, vacation villages, and other places that emphasize entertainment).[32] The heterotopia thus operates to compensate for the opening of space into infinity, one that becomes necessary as subjects come to realize that with both time and space made infinitely open there needs to be the establishment of a format through which the connection of time to space can lead to a renegotiation of the limits of space through a creative reorganization of the effects of time and place.

Heterotopias cannot exist autonomously. Foucault's fifth principle concerning heterotopias is an acknowledgment that the techniques through which heterotopias are constructed entail the use of force. Heterotopias presuppose a system of openings and closures that both isolate them and make them accessible. There are terms of permission for entry and exit, there are deceptive entries, illusive exits, there are walls that appear as doors, and windows that lead to nowhere. These constrictions are not unlike the walls of separation that serve to enclose liberal neutral spaces. Indeed, one might count the establishment of any particular zone of privacy as being a heterotopia should one work through the particularities of its place. Indeed, the last trait that Foucault identifies with heterotopias connects the idea of the heterotopia back to the more general question of freedom. He suggests that all heterotopias operate in relation to "the space that remains" in one of two ways:

> Either their role is to create a space of illusion that exposes every real space, all the sites inside of which human life is partitioned, as still more illusory (perhaps that is the role that was played by those famous brothels of which we are now deprived). Or else, on the contrary, their role is to create a space that is other, another real space, as perfect, meticulous, as well arranged as ours is messy, ill constructed, and jumbled. The latter type would be the heterotopia, not of illusion, but of compensation, and I wonder if certain colonies have not functioned somewhat in this manner. I am thinking, for example, of the first wave of colonization in the seventeenth century, of the Puritan societies that the English founded in America and were absolutely perfect other places.[33]

Foucault's intuition, expressed at the conclusion of his lecture, is that the quality of imagination in a given society is intimately related to the external organization of that society's space. The heterotopia *par excellence* is the boat, a floating space that connects all other heterotopias, linking colonies and the gardens they contain, forcing the juxtaposition of unlike elements to the end of keeping unsettled and open the possibility of new spatial arrangements. ("In civilizations without boats," he concludes, "dreams dry up, espionage takes the place of adventure, and the police take the place of pirates," p. 27).

Foucault's reference to the boat in this lecture is, of course, not the first time he thinks about the role of boats in the modern imagination. Early in his first major work, *Madness and Civilization,* Foucault also refers to a boat, the famous "Ship of Fools." Of the madman's experience on this ship he writes,

> Navigation delivers man to the uncertainty of fate; on water, each of us in the hands of his own destiny; every embarkation is, potentially, the last. It is for the other world that the madman sets sail in his fool's boat; it is from the other

world that he comes when he disembarks. The madman's voyage is at once a rigorous division and an absolute Passage. In one sense, it simply develops, across a half-real, half-imaginary geography, the madman's *liminal* position on the horizon of medieval concern—a position symbolized and made real at the same time by the madman's privilege of being confined within the city *gates*: his exclusion must enclose him; if he cannot and must not have another prison than the threshold itself, he is kept at the point of passage. He is put in the interior of the exterior, and inversely.[34]

In *Madness and Civilization,* Foucault asks why this ship came to assume such importance in the cultural landscape during this transition to the modern age. His answer: "Because it symbolized a great disquiet, suddenly dawning on the horizon of European culture at the end of the Middle Ages."[35] During this period, madness came to be comprehended as a subjective experience that must be placed outside the realm of reason. Through the strategies designed to cope with the need to establish reason as the discourse of the modern age, the imagination is itself colonized, confined, presented as an inside that is paradoxically outside of reason. This outside of reason then is locked in a struggle with the order that defines it.

The ship in this early appearance in Foucault's work is a repository of imagination and serves as an instrument that casts the experience of madness to the margins of culture. In *Madness and Civilization,* the Ship of Fools is presented as something between an allegory and a historical phenomenon. Moreover, the idea of the boat as the vehicle through which the enclosed spaces of the Middle Ages might be reinscribed, making visible the reason that was obscured by the presence of madness within city gates and correspondingly making unreason disappear from view, adumbrates a perspective on freedom that traces it to the experience of exclusion, to being thrown out of the city. (This view has been sentimentalized in various historical descriptions of the frontier experience of the European conquest of America, especially in its North American version.[36]) The idea that the location of freedom is an experience born in the margins of order is an important motif in Foucault's later work.

But Foucault's idea of the heterotopia emphasizes freedom's connection to imaginary possibilities as much as to movement through space. The heterotopia, as a site of juxtaposition in which there is contestation and struggle, exists in contrast to the empty site, the evacuated space that maintains its neutrality by evading opportunities of conflict. This latter space is that which is advocated by liberals as the best way to secure social peace. Foucault might identify in the work of some of these liberals the traces of sacred longing, a subterranean desire for ontological certainty that will eventuate (eventually) in a reaction against their rule by those who are more directly invested in preserving the face of God on earth. In this sense, Foucault's analysis of space is indebted to his understanding of the import of the death of God for the conceptualization of and political struggles over the limitlessness of space in a limited world. Heterotopias act as counters to the purity of those spaces that would operate as sacred spaces or as their secular substitutes.

So, one source of the unsettling power of heterotopias is its challenge to the sanctity of space in both its sacred and secular constructions. Another one is the disquiet concerning the role of madness in the development and articulation of imagination itself. But in his preface to *The Order of Things* (where he first discusses the idea of the heterotopia as such), Foucault presents yet another perspective on the idea of the heterotopia that, while every bit as appreciative of its power as a counter to more ordinary spaces, notes another source of disquiet, of the "uneasiness" associated with its very existence. In contrast to utopias, which operate as forms of consolation, Foucault writes,

> Heterotopias are disturbing, probably because they secretly undermine language, because they make it impossible to name this *and* that, because they shatter or tangle common names, because they destroy "syntax" in advance, and not only the syntax with which we construct sentences but also that less apparent syntax which causes words and things (next to and opposite each other) to "hold together." This is why utopias permit fables and discourse: they run with the very grain of language and are part of the fundamental dimension of the *fabula*; heterotopias . . . desiccate speech, stop words in their tracks, contest the very possibility of grammar at its source; they dissolve our myths and sterilize the lyricism of our sentences.[37]

Thus Foucault acknowledges the paradoxical force of heterotopias that prevents them from becoming "reputable." They are dangerous to the order of things, even as they are necessary to the establishment of order. And not simply the order of things, but of words as well. Heterotopias press the limits of language, demonstrate the fragility of the connection between words and things, and illustrate the forces that can be loosed when the stability of their connections is undermined by the exposure of the strategies used to subordinate one to the other. Disrupting the word's stability presses against the sacred in its more originary form, as the word as God. Sacred spaces, sacred words—both are dissolved in that high noon where everything is seen without shadow.

Disruption. The heterotopia shows the constant impossibility of closure that follows from the rise of an open and infinite space and hence the terms through which we might learn how to resist the utopian.[38] This relationship of space to its representation is an intimate one. But the terms of its intimacy are revealed by the heterotopia not to be that of a relationship of interior to exterior but of the creation of an interiority out of the infinitely open field of space. The heterotopia transgresses boundaries as a moment of freedom. The heterotopia is distinguished from other spaces in that it is the very expression of transgression. For Foucault, these moments of transgression that are shaped by and shape the heterotopia establish the "other" terms of freedom through which we might live.

Beginning with his understanding of the importance of the death of God, Foucault distinguishes himself from most contemporary thinkers, who either have attempted to solve the problems associated with religiosity by asserting the possibility that there can be a separation of a secular realm from issues of religiosity, generally achieved through the liberal separation of church and state, or have hoped that the issues associated with the religious impulse will dissipate as the force of modernity does its work to transcend the historical role of religion itself.[39] Rather than a principle of transcendence, alternatively for Foucault, "transgression is an action which involves the limit, that narrow zone of a line where it displays the flash of its passage, but perhaps also its entire trajectory, even its origin; it is likely that transgression has its entire space in the line it crosses."[40]

Foucault poses the idea of transgression in direct opposition to the idea that there can or should be a transcendence of the limits of being, suggesting that it can be understood as a new philosophical possibility, that of "nonpositive affirmation."[41] He offers transgression as an alternative to the idea that the force of sovereignty is containable and deployable by an agent who can direct it. This idea, of course, puts him in opposition to most contemporary liberals, primarily because of the element of *control* that he sees as an illusion. "Transgression," he writes, " . . .is not related to the limit as black to white, the prohibited to the lawful, the outside to the inside, or as the open area of a building to its enclosed spaces. Rather, their relationship takes the form of a spiral which no simple infraction can exhaust."[42] The connection is fleeting, "like a flash of lightning" that illuminates and then disappears into obscurity.[43]

> Transgression does not seek to oppose one thing to another, nor does it achieve its purpose through mockery or by upsetting the solidity of foundations; it does not transform the other side of the mirror, beyond an invisible and uncrossable line, into a glittering expanse. Transgression is neither violence in a divided world (in an ethical world) nor a victory over limits (in a dialectical or revolutionary world); and exactly for this reason, its role is to measure the excessive distance that it opens at the heart of the limit and to trace the flashing line that causes the limit to arise. Transgression contains nothing negative, but it affirms limited being—affirms the limitlessness into which it leaps as it opens this zone to existence for the first time. But correspondingly, this affirmation contains nothing positive: no content can bind it, since, by definition, no limit can possibly restrict it. Perhaps it is simply an affirmation of division; but only insofar as division is not understood to mean a cutting gesture, or the establishment of a separation or the measuring of a distance, only retaining that in it which may designate the existence of difference.[44]

Transgression is to be understand as a "yes," an affirmation of limited being in a limitless universe.[45] As such, it comes into being as a consequence of a shift in our understanding of the relationship of the self to the other, of the boundaries that shape our being in common and alone. Foucault understands that shift as a recircling movement, turning philosophy again toward the (pre-Socratic) Greeks but on terms that would no longer refer us back to the divinity that was the originary point of their questioning. Our references to divinity must now proceed on terms that recognize the death of God. So he is more concerned to ask what the terms of *our* questioning might be.

Foucault wants to understand this experience of the divine in such a way as to evade the brutality of the dialectic and the sterility of deontology. He sees this as possible through transgressive thought. Divinity without God is reflected in our lives through the practice of a freedom that acknowledges the finitude of being in an indefinitely infinite universe. As a precondition to knowing how we are free, transgression provides us with an alternative way of thinking through the conditions of that freedom's possibility. He writes,

No form of dialectical movement, no analysis of constitutions and their transcendental ground can serve as support for thinking about such an experience or even as access to that experience. In our day, would not the instantaneous play of the limit and of transgression be the essential test for a thought which centers on the "origin," for that form of thought to which Nietzsche dedicated us from the beginning of his works and one which would be, absolutely and in the same motion, a Critique and an Ontology, an understanding that comprehends both finitude and being?[46]

In this essay, a tribute to the work of Bataille, Foucault identifies the discourse of eroticism as that which best serves this transgressive function, the need to keep open the most important questions of being. What he describes is an eroticism that is cognizant of the fact that it is not sex itself that is at stake in the staging of transgressive acts. Whether they be the pornographic dismemberments described by Bataille or the perfectly enclosed spaces of the Marquis de Sade, the point of such enactments is to demonstrate the limits of our language so as to allow us to know how to traverse the boundaries of experience.

The spaces of heterotopias are informed by the transgressions of their boundaries, by the enunciations they encourage and the contradictions they incite. We can see the effects of them everywhere we choose to look, but the question for us is whether we will so choose. The boundaries of our experiences do not limit us so much as outline the trajectory of our being. We do not evade politics by trying to preserve a pure space of the apolitical. Indeed, the politics that proceed in such places are sometimes the worse for it. Such a politics presents us with restraints upon our desires to transgress, restraints that are constructed with the barely obscured purpose of allowing us to kill in the name of a higher principle. We might instead seek to open up the realm of our experience to other conditions that will loosen the restraints we find ourselves imposing upon our selves and our ways of being free. And the conditions that will allow freer experiences to occur? We might know, with Foucault, that there is no pure imagination that will release us from the constraints of our lives. We can be assured, however, that there are ways available to us to be free and that our freedom is not to be confined by the limits we have imposed upon it in the name of such pure ends, even though such freedom is to be defined by them.

The Neutral Space of Negative Freedom

What is the space of freedom? Isaiah Berlin begins his essay "Two Concepts of Liberty" with the now famous observation that there are essentially two kinds of freedom: negative and positive.[47]

> The first of these political senses of freedom or liberty (I shall use both words to mean the same), which (following much precedent) I shall call the "negative" sense, is involved in the answer to the question, "What is the area within which the subject—a person or group of persons—is or should be left to do or be what he is able to do or be, without interference from other persons?" The second, which I shall call the positive sense, is involved in the answer to the question, "What, or who, is the source of control or interference that can determine someone to do, or be, this rather than that?" The two questions are clearly different, even though the answers to them may overlap.[48]

In presenting this dual formulation of freedom Berlin claims that he "follows much precedent." He is right. Indeed, in large part, the power of Berlin's essay derives from its extraordinarily synthetic quality. His most explicit categories are rooted in the familiar, in that they refer to concepts that compose the ordinary language of political philosophers. He writes of doing and being, of agency and result, of persons and subjects. He actively seeks the familiar, even allowing freedom and liberty to be used as synonyms. He discusses freedom in relationship to the most compelling desires of the age, humanizing as he opposes those who seek freedom in ways other than through the means he believes it to be best realized. His rhetoric of freedom is profoundly appealing, in that it suggests that Berlin is attuned to particularity, to the ordinary sites through which freedom is expressed.

The familiar is present in Berlin's essay in a more subtle sense as well. Perhaps most compelling about his formulation of the meanings of freedom is how he imagines a kind of ever-present presence, a stability provided by the inarticulate role of neutral space as the ground of both negative and positive freedom. Berlin calls it "area," or "frontier"[49] or "portion," or "sphere."[50] It is worth noting though, that in all cases the space he designates as a site of freedom is natural, not constructed, either invaded or evacuated, empty or filled, cultivated or wild. In contrast to Foucault, Berlin's epistemological assumption concerning space is that it *is of itself:*

as an empty neutrality, space operates as the *ground* upon which his argument concerning freedom is constructed, and as the product of the boundaries that produce it, space is the container for freedom, that which protects it as a possession of the boundaries created by its own exercise.

The idea of space as a neutral place is for most liberal thinkers an obvious banality and a not so obvious source of anxiety. To assert that freedom is comprehensible primarily in reference to a space assumed to be neutral betrays the inherent instability of neutral space when imposed as an absolute category. This instability is a consequence of the always politically ambiguous achievement of spatial neutrality. In presenting space as neutral, Berlin makes it the ground of freedom. To establish this space as the ground is to render it outside of contestation or struggle. Space is uncontestable as a neutral ground to the extent that one is prevented from questioning its production or recognizing that the production of space is always already an architectural enterprise. But when one remembers that space itself is produced, or, more provocatively, insists upon investigating the ways in which it is produced, one is better able to see the manner in which the neutrality of space operates as an architectural metaphor for grounding. In making this recognition, one might be able to see how political philosophy displaces an important dimension of itself in its attempts to render itself nonmetaphorical.[51] As Mark Wigley comments in regard to philosophy more generally, "The figure of a building as a grounded structure cannot be discarded to reveal any fundamental ground, as the sense of 'fundamental' is produced by that very figure."[52] So while Berlin is able to assert that negative freedom is inexorably associated with "non-interference" within a space, he leaves the politics of the architecture and construction of space unquestioned.

Moreover, if one accepts, with Foucault, that transgressions are themselves practical exercises of freedom, the containment of freedom in neutral space becomes incoherent. From this perspective, the very establishment of the terms of neutrality arises from situations that are themselves not neutral but are, instead, locations of struggles to evade harm and instantiate desire. One needs to ask, what struggles, what desires, are constitutive of liberal spaces of freedom?

By displacing questions concerning how space is established through processes that are intrinsically political, by burying them in the foundation, so to speak, Berlin is able to achieve definitional clarity in the Nietzschean sense of denying its definition any history. The *meaning* of freedom is minimized, as a reflection of the desire of those who seek to make freedom a controllable entity, who seek to make freedom synonymous with control. Negative freedom means to be left alone: the more one is left alone the freer one becomes.

> The criterion of oppression is the part that I believe is directly played by other human beings, directly or indirectly, with or without the intention of doing so, in frustrating my wishes. By being free in this sense I mean not being interfered with by others. The wider the area of non-interference the wider my freedom.[53]

One is free in a negative sense because one's ability to act must be a movement *away from* those forces that hold one in place, into the neutral space assumed to be outside of power. Although there will be occasions and situations when it will inevitably be necessary to curtail freedom (for the sake of preserving it), there is an irreducible minimum space of freedom for individuals that must not be violated for the condition of negative freedom to exist at all. This minimum area of freedom is protected by the legal enunciation of liberal rights. The boundaries of politics are established as the lines drawn by law: they allow interventions into neutral space only to protect the ground of freedom and usually protect the exercise of freedom simply by prohibiting interventions, as a great no. "A frontier must be drawn between the area of private life and that of public authority. Where it is to be drawn is a matter of argument, indeed of haggling."[54]

In this formulation Berlin does not question how authority is created to direct the positive powers required to produce the neutral space within which one freely acts.[55] But even before he reaches that part of his discussion, Berlin establishes as axiomatic that negative freedom is an absolute value, that is, a value not capable of exchange from one agent to another but, instead, unalienable from the agent who has it. This absolute character of negative freedom is entailed in the more overt claims that he makes concerning the noncommensurability of certain values. He writes, in discussing the question of sacrificing freedom,

> Everything is what it is: liberty is liberty, not equality or fairness or justice or culture, or human happiness or a quiet conscience. If the liberty of myself or my class or nation depends on the misery of a number of other human beings,

the system which promotes this is unjust and immoral. But if I curtail or lose my freedom, in order to lessen the shame of such inequality, and do not thereby materially increase the individual liberty of others, an absolute loss of liberty occurs. This may be compensated for by a gain in justice or in happiness or in peace, but the loss remains, and it is a confusion of values to say that although my "liberal" individual freedom may go by the board, some other kind of freedom—"social" or "economic" is increased.[56]

In short, negative freedom is not fungible, or to be negative, it must be made unfungible. Negative freedom is not rooted in exchange, in compromise, in anything other than the agency of the individual. That agency is not secondhand but is, instead, carefully cultivated within each free person, which is why Berlin is cautious in advocating the sacrifice of individual negative freedom as a strategy for rectifying injustices or to diminish the shame of inequality, even if that inequality might be associated with the exercise of negative freedom in the first place.

Negative freedom taken by itself, however, is problematic for Berlin, precisely because by itself it is not incompatible with some forms of autocratic rule. "Liberty in this sense is principally concerned with the area of control, not with its source."[57] The difficulty of negative freedom is that it is not logically connected with democracy or self-government. Berlin sees the need to synthesize that connection as the raison d'être of positive freedom. If one is to determine the grounds of freedom, one must move on to ask about the status of the agent. The question of agency involves the determination of the subject who is to bear the absolute right of freedom or who is to have that right taken away. The line of inquiry into the status of the subject as agent has informed a great deal of contemporary discussion of liberal freedom. It is a primary ground of contestation between contemporary liberals and communitarians.[58] But, as Bonnie Honig points out, while liberals and communitarians alike will concede that the self as an autonomous agent may well be situated, both groups are deeply resistant to contemplating the idea that the self may be produced.[59] While there is a history to this resistance, in that liberal theorists have in the past identified their enemy as those who adhere to a positivist behavioralism, their common reluctance to discuss the question of the constitution of the agent is most fundamentally associated with their desire to limit political contestation, as Honig persuasively argues. An element of that reluctance, an element that still distinguishes some liberals from most communitarians, stems from a liberal determination that the constitution of selves is a process that rightly, fundamentally, must belong outside the domain of public authority, within the "inner ocean" of the self. (Most contemporary communitarians externalize that authority more easily, either explicitly or implicitly identifying the source of their authority as a god who sets in motion a law they can know and act upon. In this, they act in the tradition of positive freedom when it is most clearly attached to natural law. But although they may think they have succeeded in evading this problem by dint of their secularism, the question of god is not evaded by liberalism simply by setting it aside, as we will see below.)

Because the self is the bearer of fundamental rights, liberals are deeply uneasy when the individual is characterized in such ways as to lessen his or her dignity and autonomy or when the integrity of agentic autonomy is challenged by perspectives that emphasize the conditions that cultivate that agency or may even emphasize that the status of the agent is intimately tied to the capacity for self-rule. But he also knows that the instruments of self-rule are not located exclusively within the agent. He understands them to concern the second side of freedom, positive freedom. Positive freedom is initially derived from the wish to be one's own master.

> I wish to be an instrument of my own, not of other men's acts of will. I wish to be a subject, not an object; to be moved by reasons, by conscious purposes, which are my own, not by causes which affect me, as it were, from the outside. I wish to be somebody, not nobody; a doer—deciding, not being decided for, self-directed and not acted upon by external nature or by other men as though I were a thing, or an animal, or a slave incapable of playing a human role, that is, of conceiving goals and policies of my own and realizing them.[60]

This wish is a source of great danger because it establishes a minimal precondition for understanding the self who is to be ruled as being (at least) bifurcated, as having higher and lower aspects. Self-mastery straightforwardly implies that there is a willful self to be mastered by a better self. Appeals made to the higher element of the self can lead to the establishment of tyrannies worse than autocracy. Berlin writes,

> The 'positive' conception of freedom as self-mastery, with its suggestion of a man divided against himself, has, in fact, and as a matter of history, of doctrine and practice, lent itself more easily to this splitting of personality in

two: the transcendent, dominant controller, and the empirical bundle of desires and passions to be disciplined and brought to heel.[61]

For Berlin, there have been two major alternative ways of being free available to people who pursue the desire to be self-directed; first, a pursuit of inner freedom through self-abnegation, and second, a self-identification with a larger ideal, a projection of the self into the world. The former movement consists of embracing the idea of freedom as obedience to a law of one's own making; the latter is the process of identifying oneself with a larger law of reason one has discovered or has been shown. He identifies the former with Kant and the latter with Marx, although eventually, he suggests, even highly individualist thinkers like Kant were to come to the point of asking whether a rational life could be made possible for all of society and hence could be considered as more akin to the sort of rationalism practiced by Marxists.[62] The doctrine of such a rationalism is straightforward.

> The common assumption of these thinkers (and of many a schoolman before them and Jacobin and Communist after them) is that the rational ends of our "true" natures must coincide, or be made to coincide, however violently our poor, ignorant, desire-ridden, passionate empirical selves may cry out against this process.[63]

Identification with a law of reason is complicated by what Berlin calls the "search for status."[64] When one realizes the embeddedness of the agent within a society, often the desire for freedom, especially positive freedom, is confused with the desire for recognition.[65] The desire for recognition underwrites nationalist aspirations, but it also responds to something more. Berlin notes,

> This wish to assert the "personality" of my class, or group or nation, is connected both with the answer to the question, "What is to be the area of authority?" (for the group must not be interfered with by outside masters), and even more closely, with the answer to the question "Who is to govern us?" —govern well or badly, liberally or oppressively—but above all "who?"[66]

For Berlin, the answer to the question concerning who will rule is separable from the question of freedom itself.

Provided the answer to "Who shall govern me?" is somebody or something which belongs to me, or to whom I belong, I can, by using words which convey fraternity and solidarity, as well as some part of the connotation of the "positive" sense of the word freedom (which it is difficult to specify more precisely), describe it as a hybrid form of freedom; at any rate as an ideal which is perhaps more prominent than any other in the world today, yet one which no preexisting term seems to fit.[67]

The more general question that energizes contemporary debates concerning the relationship of group identity to freedom is, in Berlin's argument, immediately related to the interior boundaries of agency. His phrase "somebody or something which belongs to me, or to whom I belong" emphasizes this connection and shows the limits of thinking about this hybrid as a kind of freedom at all because the reversal of belonging refers one to the absorption of identity into a claim of universal right.

Between these two forces militating against negative freedom—rationalism and group identity—Berlin locates the force of sovereignty. If the claims of group identity present a connecting link between the psychological underpinnings of agency and the demands of positive freedom, and if rationalism identifies a form of rule that will submerge the individual agent in a larger commonality, the abiding form of the link between individual and polity is the issuance of sovereignty, which is the public power to interfere in the lives of individual citizens. The link provided by sovereignty is that of final authority: it connects these divergent impulses and at the same time operates slightly outside of and above them. In part because sovereignty answers the question concerning who has authority over agents, the issue concerning sovereignty moves to that of how much power is to be wielded over citizens. Sovereignty is thus the opposite of negative freedom, challenging the autonomy of the agents under its rule. It is dangerous to negative freedom because "the sovereignty of the people [can] easily destroy that of individuals."[68]

Berlin believes that critics of sovereignty too often misconstrue the problem posed by the exercise of positive liberty by seeing the problem of sovereignty as being that of who governs rather than seeing it as a question of "the accumulation of power itself."[69] But for him there is another aspect of sovereignty that does not entail the destruction of individuality so much as it threatens the outside limits of its existence. Liberals must engage in the exercise of positive liberty for one reason, and one reason only; to protect the absolute values of negative liberty.[70] Liberals, that is, those who understand negative liberty as an absolute right, will participate in government with an eye toward limiting its power; others, the opponents of liberalism, will participate in government in order to expand it, setting as higher values other than negative liberty.[71] Berlin asserts that the latter seek, beyond justice, beyond progress, or the happiness of future generations, confirmation of a belief, "that somewhere . . . there is a final solution."[72]

Berlin's critique here parallels Foucault, to the extent that it acknowledges the consequences that the assertion of an infinitely open (and hence uncertain) space has on the certitude of higher values. Against the desire to confirm the belief in a final and certain solution to problems, Berlin poses the openness that is the core ethic of the liberal tradition. In response to the dangers posed by sovereignty, and the always present danger that no democracy is disqualified from the possibility of abrogating liberal rights, he suggests that the liberal response must be to resist. He identifies two principles fundamental to a liberal society:

> First, that no power, but only rights, can be regarded as absolute, so that all men, whatever power governs them, have an absolute right to refuse to behave inhumanly; and, second, that there should be frontiers, not artificially drawn, within which men should be inviolable, these frontiers being defined in terms of rules so long and so widely accepted that their observance has entered into the very conception of what it means to be a normal human being, and therefore, also of what it is to act inhumanly or insanely: rules of which it would be absurd to say, for example, that they could be abrogated by some formal procedure on the part of some court or sovereign body. . . . The freedom of a society, or a class or a group, in this sense of freedom, is measured by the strength of these barriers, and the number and importance of the paths which they keep open for their members—if not for all, for at any rate a great number of them.[73]

But ironically, or perhaps, most appropriately, it is here, in the crucible of negative freedom, where Berlin evokes core principles of liberalism, that one finds evidence of a particular working of power, albeit one that goes unacknowledged by him. This is the work done by the force of the normal.

Berlin moves the normal to the foundation of "what it means to be a human being."[74] By making this move he evades an important question concerning how the idea of the normal itself operates as a form of power.

This evasion is not merely incidental to his purposes but essential to his argument concerning negative liberty because it turns out that the need for a ground that will not be questioned requires not only neutral space but solid and (relatively) unambiguous human beings to fill those neutral spaces. He asserts that the frontiers created out of human usage "are not artificially drawn." It is as though the inviolability of right is a *natural* fact and not achieved through the very processes he describes in the same sentence. It is as though the penetration of rules that define our humanity, the violence, the struggle, the costs in blood and memory are to be, however honorable the intention, removed from the field of contestation and struggle, rhetorically protected through the evocation of "natural," repressively wrenched from their situatedness in the lives of those who puzzle through who and how they are in the world, and placed beyond violence, struggle, blood, and memory. The heart of negative liberty is a space of agency, protected against the vicissitudes of political sovereigns by a reversion to a discipline so deep and powerful as to make real the illusion of a human being who exists beyond artifice.

Here Berlin succumbs to the temptation, born of a horrible knowledge of the dangers associated with exploring the ground upon which the standards of humanity are built, to revert to the absolute categories of which he is justly suspicious. Asserting that "the normal is the natural" places the liberal project at risk because it elevates liberal values in the same way that those who elevate positive freedom do, using essentially the same instruments of power. Moreover, Berlin immediately sacrifices some of the agents who are to be saved. He insists that the achievement of the normal depends upon the establishment of barriers that, while keeping paths open to freedom for some members of a polity, do not do so for all. Berlin does not suggest that membership itself is limited and does not even suggest that a majority of members of a society will enjoy freedom in the manner he suggests but only that through the art of separation "a great number of [the members of a society]" will enjoy freedom. The barriers that establish inviolability, then, do not even succeed for everyone. Although a liberal, Berlin is no democrat in this sense.

But in a more insidious sense he is. Normality is an operation that depends on separating majorities from minorities. It establishes heterotopias of deviance as a primary device for establishing neutrality as the norm, as the governing principle for all in a liberal social order. The work of the normal gives a solidity to agents that they otherwise would not have by distributing them in space around a predefined norm. The ideal of the normal enables its agents not to question the ground of their self-existence as political beings. Normalcy, coupled with the wall of privacy secured by the practices establishing the neutral space of negative liberty, enables all sorts of practical exercises of power that will shape and discipline selves into inviolable human beings. In securing the grounds of the self by elevating its humanity to a natural status, one is able to displace the politics of self-constitution, putting the practices of the normal at a remove from the issues that our common sense once told us should address the sovereign powers of positive freedom.

The proliferation of normalcy is a confinement of freedom enabled by the very evasion of the politics entailed in the construction of space as neutral. Normalcy becomes the silent arbitrator of the normative. It exposes the agent who bears liberal rights as someone who evades a confrontation with the various forces of morality and immorality by sticking to the straight and narrow of the norm. This choice is made inevitable by the liberal evasion of a confrontation with sacred power through the establishment of the division of public and private realms of existence. That split will continually hold out as a threat what could otherwise be comprehended as a promise: the possibility of a transgression of both good and evil. The contingent character of life and its finitude thus can be brought into the service of control over agency rather than becoming an instrument for the transgression of the limits of normalcy.

Such an agent will indeed complement the neutral space it is to inhabit. Neutral space will enable one to act politically in the public realm while repressing challenges to political action that emanate from the unruly realm of the private. A whole range of matters can then be dismissed by being said to be unpolitical or insufficiently political. Such matters might include questions of race, gender, sexuality, ethnic identity, family structure, class, and criminality, all the forces that Berlin sees as threats to negative freedom save one—rationalism. Rationalism requires direct confrontation and negotiation, because it is the method through which the sovereign power of the modern state operates. But from the normal perspective of negative liberty, these other forces are but atavistic irrationalities. They must be confined and subordinated, but the way in which they will be confined and subordinated must not be connected to the more explicit exercises of positive freedom. Instead, the work of the normal operates to constitute their humanity. And with the field cleared of the messy terms of engagement entailed by the processes of the constitution of identity, the security of negative freedom will be more or less achieved.

So Berlin sees no alternative but for liberals to secure the ground of negative freedom by making human beings inviolable. In doing so, he implicitly makes the same concession that he sees Kant making when connecting the conditions of inner freedom to those required of an order based on reason. But for Berlin it is freedom, not reason, that is both the end and means of political action. The inviolability that he insists must be naturalized secures the ground of the pluralism entailed by that freedom. And it is this pluralism he invokes as the best means of negotiating cultural conflict. But how can such a pluralism, as limited as it is by its normalized confinement, aid in such a negotiation? The means through which such an inviolable status is to be achieved, a position from which one can *refuse* to behave in an inhuman way, reveals the shortcomings of both the goal and the means to achieve it. In establishing inviolability as a consequence of the achievement of the normal, Berlin moves a practice of positive freedom into the heart of the negative freedom that is to be protected from sovereign power. In surrounding conventions of the normal with the aura of inviolability, Berlin quietly posits a conventional positive freedom from which negative freedom proceeds and which positive freedom contains. He would raise a set of all-too-human practices to a standing independent of their history because he cannot imagine the refusal to act inhumanly to be based on anything other than practices that themselves must go unquestioned. To acknowledge that these practices have a history would be to admit that they might someday disappear and with them the humanity that is the end of them. In other words, it would seem, from Berlin's perspective, that to question one's humanity is to succumb to the very forces that negative liberty opposes.

Berlin breaches the wall between public and private in the name of asserting the priority of private humanity over public good. In its decrepit form, this breach underlies many other breaches—in the areas of public education, religious freedom, morality, and racial relations. Acts of breaching lead to a heightened reliance on the juridical concept of substantive due process and, more generally, to the clamoring for rights and entitlements as weapons in a world of competing and conflicting rights. Yet Berlin's insistence on the inviolability of human beings allows each breach of the wall to exist as an exception to the rule: in the preface and aftermath of each violation of the inviolably human, the liberal will reassert the always already present division between public authority and private right. But it is the inviolable and its violation *together* that define the practice of negative liberty. This formulation of inviolability is not a cynical gesture. It comes straight from the sentimental heart of liberalism itself, the desire to minimize cruelty, to do as little harm as is possible to other human beings.

Berlin is a bleeding heart liberal, in the best sense of the term. But his liberalism is enabled nonetheless by that which he would deny. Although the neutral space of negative freedom is heterotopic in character, open to transgression, the style of transgression that Berlin seems to advocate does not acknowledge itself as transgressive action at all but, rather, as a series of privileged exceptions to an unviolable right.

Establishing human inviolability through the elevation of the normal, Berlin enables pluralism to operate in a manner compatible with the skepticism and insecurity associated with the exercise of negative freedom. He writes, "Pluralism, with the measure of 'negative liberty' that it entails, seems to me a truer and more humane ideal than those who seek in the great, disciplined, authoritarian structures the ideal of 'positive' self-mastery by classes, or peoples, or the whole of mankind."[75] Here, Berlin is able to have his ideal and eat it too. Berlin insists that this ideal is elusive, ambiguous, and ephemeral. But for him there can be no other. He concludes his essay with this complex and elusive enunciation:

> It may be that the ideal of freedom to choose ends without claiming eternal validity for them, and the pluralism of values connected with this, is only the late fruit of our declining capitalist civilization: an ideal which remote ages and primitive societies have not recognized, and one which posterity will regard with curiosity, even sympathy, but little comprehension. This may be so: but no skeptical conclusions seem to me to follow. Principles are not less sacred because their duration cannot be guaranteed. Indeed, the very desire for guarantees that our values are eternal and secure in some objective heaven is perhaps only a craving for the certainties of childhood or the absolute values of our primitive past. "To realize the relative validity of one's convictions," said an admirable writer of our time, "and yet stand for them unflinchingly, is what distinguishes a civilized man from a barbarian." To demand more than this is perhaps a deep and incurable metaphysical need: but to allow it to determine one's practice is a symptom of an equally deep, and more danger-ous, moral and political immaturity.[76]

Berlin here rehistoricizes that which he had earlier attempted to place outside of history. But this rehistoricization of liberal values reinforces his argument, because for Berlin an uncertain redemption lies between the past and future. Moreover, in the light of history the very ephemerality of liberal values makes them more precious, "sacred" even.

An even more complex and paradoxical argument unfolds in the final three sentences of his essay. Here Berlin exemplifies the position of the post-World War II, Cold War liberal. One must stand for one's values, even though one may know them only to be relatively valid, because the alternative is relatively worse.[77] (It is the absolutism of Nazism and Communism that one must fear, not the putative nihilism they are now said to reflect, as contemporary conservatives would falsely reconstruct this political history.) But such a liberalism is dependent upon (and relieved of an important responsibility by) a reading of the permanence of a "metaphysical need" for certainty, or for a final solution to the problems facing humankind. Liberalism will oppose this moral and political immaturity, will in fact place this metaphysical need against its aspirations. What this form of liberalism cannot do, however, is question the ways in which it is implicated in the immaturity it opposes. Behind the ramparts of inviolable agency, within the neutral space in which such agents act, those who hold to the ideal of negative liberty deploy pluralism as a contemporary strategy of toleration. But liberal pluralism, as it is connected to negative liberty, denies its agents the capacity to think through the conditions that establish its own metaphysical needs. Thus the irony of Berlin's embrace of pluralism is that even this one anchor of negative liberty, in the normal creation of "the natural," may too firmly secure the grounds of negative freedom, preventing its exercise as a concrete practice. Pluralism on these terms may be permissible only for those who will not exercise it (as is demonstrated by the rise of new fundamentalisms of the late twentieth century in the wake of the death of God).

Within the framework of Berlin's historical understanding, the rise and fall of negative liberty, the building and demolition of the walls and bridges of modern freedom, and the possibility for achieving a freedom that will be pure as a consequence of its establishment through the segregation of space are all revealed as the fragile processes of contingency that they are, dependent upon forces that may turn on them. But this characterization of Berlin is, of course, not quite as he would have it. He sees his work as constructive, not destructive. But he also sees history's possibilities in more restrictive terms than does Foucault because he is convinced that the range of freedom is more limited than does Foucault, necessarily restricted as it is by the normal, and based upon a common sense and a range of experience that is necessarily only mediated by the rules that determine one's maturity.[78]

Where Berlin would see the loss of specifically sanctified spaces as a gain for freedom and the rise of more general principles of spaces of deviance as simply consistent with the neutrality of modern space's maturity, Foucault might suggest that such presumptions are problematic in that the loss entailed in the proliferation of heterotopias of deviance that are designed to secure the normal is also loss of a particular kind of heterogeneously free space—that is, space that by the very richness of the imaginary juxtapositions it affords is free. Moreover, the reduction of the exercise of freedom to a heteronomously free space—that is, to a space that is only secondhandedly free, free in contrast to and by virtue of its submission to external principles of governing legitimacy—is paradoxically free only to the extent that its governing principles are free. And since those governing principles are rooted in a desire to provide coherence and clarity, we never move to a more robust, or in Foucault's terms, concrete space of freedom. In that sense, Berlin's attempt to establish a secular freedom fails because it relies on the persistence of a space that is not desanctified.[79] The style of transgression that knows itself as such is more available as an experience of freedom under circumstances in which space is open, desanctified. Such a spatial situation would produce a pluralism that might be a more robust alternative to the liberalism of negative freedom espoused by Berlin. Such a transgression operates in the face of a more profound historicization than Berlin is willing to confront in his work.

What confrontation does Berlin avoid? What does he remain silent about? No more and no less than the death of God. Foucault, having learned from Nietzsche the perils of evading the death of God, will not shrink from this thought and its implications. "The death of God," he writes, "does not restore us to a limited and positivistic world, but to a world exposed by the experience of its limits, made and unmade by that excess which transgresses it."[80] Berlin tries to evade the consequences of the death of God by asserting a humanism—inviolable humanity—that ultimately varies only in emphasis from the rationalism he sees at the heart of positive freedom. The positivity at the core of Berlin's assertion of the inviolably human rigidifies the boundaries of the human, which Foucault believes is the greater danger facing us. We cannot pretend that the world can be resolved, even in the limited sense that Berlin is tempted to give us (and himself). To do so heightens our peril by pretending that we are as infinite as the space we inhabit. It gives us one more excuse for being violent in the name of good. Berlin's expressed desire to naturalize the practices that disallow the inhuman treatment of other humans becomes ashes in his mouth. His wish goes with the grain of the utopian: the practices that will allow his wish to come into being make his desire into a claim continuous with the wish of those he would otherwise resist.

Berlin's liberalism, rooted in negative liberty, deliberately fragile in its commitment to a pluralism that acknowledges its relativity and its limited right to assert its grounds, is an attempt to resolve liberalism's dilemma through the displacement of one of its most important constitutive elements: space. Berlin's brilliance does not extend to an analysis of the paradoxes entailed in such a displacement, but this is not surprising. Until recently, liberalism is as liberalism does. Or, more precisely, from its emergence in the seventeenth century, liberalism has proceeded through the pretense of grounding its values in the security of neutral space and solid agents. It has done so because to do otherwise has been unimaginable for liberals, unimaginable because the experience of concrete freedom is associated exclusively for them with the most atavistic forces of theocratic religion, the residue of which can be found in positive freedom. But at the turn of the twenty-first century we have accumulated perhaps too many experiences not to be able, indeed, not to be *compelled* to imagine a more problematical rendering of the ethics of liberalism and its manner of establishing spatial relationships.

We can ask: What happens when the grounds of liberalism are exposed? Does it make a difference to how we understand our present? I believe it does, and I would make an assertion. If Freud achieved his status as a major thinker of the twentieth century by exposing the agents who bear rights as achieving this status through processes of desire below the threshold of conscious thought and action, Foucault might be said to have taken the next step.[81] Foucault exposes the contingent and open character of both the agents who bear rights and the space they inhabit so as to allow for the development of new ethical practices. Some will surely object. In what way does the work of either Freud or Foucault contribute to the understanding of freedom? Indeed, one might think—many do—that the issues that each of them in turn has raised should not be considered, that they are in fact inimical to the real study of freedom. Perhaps, as Berlin might claim, they are the practitioners of a merely "imaginary science."[82] But unlike Berlin, we might think of this term nonpejoratively, by asking if it is valuable for there to be imaginary sciences, understood not, as Berlin's context would suggest, as fanciful ravings but as attempts to comprehend the role of imagination in human endeavor. As a scientist of the imaginary, Foucault enriches our sense of freedom by showing how the constitution of its space is intimately connected to the practice of being free. We might begin to investigate this space, its pluralization, its fracturing into incommensurable and yet connected sites, and ask how it can be traversed by invoking Foucault's critique of normalization. Although that critique emerged as an explicit theme later in his thought, it is a consequence of his earlier analysis of space. In his approach to questions of space, Foucault prepares us to understand sovereignty and rights as the mutual expressions of the limits of freedom when freedom is enabled by the displacement of space.

* * *

The underwriting conditions of liberalism, even a chastened liberalism —as is Berlin's—are dependent upon an ordinary and massive displacement of the constitutive grounding through which freedom is to be realized. In making the exercise of freedom proceed from within a stable and neutral space, liberalism seeks a peace. Indeed, one way of reading the liberal tradition is as a means of escape from the turmoil associated with political life. But those who read liberalism in this way, whether hostile to what they see as an antipolitical bias in liberalism or celebratory of liberalism's suspicion of politics because of its violence, must see the strategies of liberalism as somehow not being political in and of themselves. Foucault allows us to understand the politics of liberalism in a more expansive manner, not simply through his assertions concerning how power and knowledge are mutually constituted,[83] but by his way of seeing how the organization of space itself involves a remarkable and ingenious political imagination. If we come to understand the neutral space of liberalism as the product of this powerful imagination, we might better know how the practice of freedom might be realized under the conditions of the future.

I consider it an extraordinarily fortuitous matter that Foucault's most comprehensive articulation of how we might be free can be found in his study on the modern soul, *Discipline and Punish.* I turn to that study next to retrace the steps through which sovereignty lent itself to the development of a system of rights and how that system itself is connected to the discipline that is the hallmark of modern civilization. In doing so, I hope to demonstrate that Foucault seeks, in his reconstruction of the history of our present, not to endorse a totalistic rejection of modernity but to shed light on other ways of becoming who we are. Although I realize that this depiction of Foucault's effort is not in keeping with how his work has been received, especially by those who think that an analysis launched at such a level of intensity as that of Foucault must be a "total" critique and by those who simply want to preserve a form of liberal innocence, I find it the only depiction that is consistent with the complexity of his analysis and the best way to explain his continued effort to understand the ways in which we are free.

Notes

1. See Jeff Hurn for Trimble Navigation, *GPS: A Guide to the Next Utility* (Sunnyvale, CA: Trimble Navigation, 1989), 2. The cost of the GPS, borne by the U.S. government, was $12 billion. "But it's money well spent because the system really works" (p. 7).

2. *You Are Here: Information Drift,* an installation at the Storefront for Art and Architecture, New York, NY, March 1994. See also Laura Kurgan, "You Are Here," *Documents,* nos. 1-2 (Fall/Winter 1992): 53-7.

3. One might question whether this space is, in fact, a cyberspace. The term *cyberspace* was first coined by William Gibson in his science fiction novel, *Neuromancer* (New York: Ace Books, 1984), to characterize the re-creation of three-dimensional spatial relations through visual, aural, and tactile simulations. The space created by the GPS does not depend on any of these techniques to achieve its effect. It can be characterized as a cyberspace, however, in that it (1) exists as a consequence of the will of its subjects to act as though its exists and (2) comes into being as a result of the technological extension of familiar human capacities. On this second element, see Donna Haraway, *Simians, Cyborgs, and Women: The Reinvention of Nature* (New York: Routledge, 1991), "A Cyborg Manifesto."

4. For an important analysis of how the intensification of claims to national identities operate in opposition to other, less identity-driven movements in late modernity, see William E. Connolly, "Democracy and Territoriality," in Frederick Dolan and Thomas L. Dumm, eds.,

Rhetorical Republic: Governing Representations in American Politics (Amherst: University of Massachusetts Press, 1993).

5. See Hannah Arendt, *The Human Condition* (Chicago: University of Chicago Press, 1958), 1-2.

6. For a provocative analysis of Arendt in reference to postmodernism, see Dana Villa, "Postmodernism and the Public Sphere," in Dolan and Dumm, eds., *Rhetorical Republic,* 227-48.

7. Among the works by Foucault one might consider in this regard are *The Order of Things: An Archaeology of the Human Sciences* (New York: Random House, 1970), *The Archaeology of Knowledge,* trans. Alan Sheridan-Smith (New York: Random House, 1972), *This Is Not a Pipe,* trans. James Harkness (Berkeley: University of California Press, 1983), and "Of Other Spaces," trans. Jay Misoweic, in *diacritics,* Spring 1986, 22-7. A variety of works by geographers, architects, literary theorists, and philosophers might be understood as responses to the interventions into the thinking about space that Foucault's work represents. I would include among these Edward Soja, *Postmodern Geographies: The Reassertion of Space in Critical Social Theory* (London: Verso, 1989), David Harvey, *The Condition of Postmodernity* (New York: Basil Blackwell, 1989), Henri Lefebvre, *The Production of Space* (New York: Basil Blackwell, 1991), and Edward S. Casey, *Getting Back into Place* (Bloomington: University of Indiana Press, 1993).

8. See Jane Gaines, *Contested Culture: The Image, the Voice, and the Law* (Chapel Hill: University of North Carolina Press, 1991).

9. I want to do this as a preface to showing how Foucault traces the destruction of a particular kind of space that has enabled the liberal enunciation of freedom to be.

10. See Isaiah Berlin, *Four Essays on Liberty* (Oxford: Oxford University Press, 1969), esp. "Two Concepts of Liberty."

11. This complication, while akin to the ideas concerning a Wittgensteinian-inspired "situatedness" that inform Richard Flathman's arguments about the politics of freedom, varies from Flathman's characterization in that Foucault emphasizes the way in which the external, that is, spatial, dimension of the situation of freedom is decisive in the formation of the internal, metaphorical expression of it. See Richard Flathman, *The Philosophy and Politics of Freedom* (Chicago: University of Chicago Press, 1987).

12. For an important exception to this view, see Georges Canguilhem, "On *Histoire de la folie* as an Event," *Critical Inquiry* 21: 2 (Winter 1995), 283-287.

13. For a discussion of danger, see Thomas L. Dumm, *Democracy and Punishment: Disciplinary Origins of the United States* (Madison: University of Wisconsin Press, 1987).

14. I see this problem as a flaw in the otherwise sensitive and compelling arguments of liberals such as Richard Flathman and George Kateb.

15. Foucault, *The Archaeology of Knowledge,* 211.

16. Foucault, *The Order of Things,* xxiv.

17. Ibid., 387.

18. Ibid., 15.

19. Foucault, "Of Other Spaces," 22. This lecture was presented after the publication of *The Order of Things* and prior to the publication of *The Archaeology of Knowledge.* It marks, along with a discussion of politics (which appears in the conclusion of *The Archaeology* in abbreviated form), a transition in Foucault's self-understanding of the political implications of his work. For the expanded version of Foucault's comments that appear in the conclusion of *The Archaeology of Knowledge,* see Foucault, "Politics and the Study of Discourse," trans. Colin Gordon, in Graham Burchell, Colin Gordon, and Peter Miller, eds., *The Foucault Effect:*

Studies in Governmentality (Chicago: University of Chicago Press, 1991). For a valuable chronological bibliography of Foucault's work, see James Bernauer and Thomas Keenan, "The Works of Michel Foucault, 1954-1984," in James Bernauer and David Rasmussen, eds., *The Final Foucault* (Cambridge: MIT Press, 1988), 119-166.

20. This is one explanation as to why Foucault resisted the appellation "structuralist." He understood the work that he did, which was identified as structuralism, to be an analysis of the conditions of the emergence of structural stabilities and discontinuities, but he never thought that once those were identified they would remain unchanged by that identification.

21. Ibid., 23.

22. Ibid.

23. As quoted in Ronald Hayman, *Brecht: A Biography* (Oxford: Oxford University Press, 1983), 214.

24. For an exhaustive study of the emergence of modernity that touches on these themes, see Hans Blumenberg, *The Legitimacy of the Modern Age,* trans. Robert M. Wallace (Cambridge: MIT Press, 1983).

25. Foucault, "Of Other Spaces," 23.

26. Ibid.

27. Ibid., 24.

28. Ibid.

29. Ibid., 25.

30. Ibid.

31. Ibid.

32. Ibid., 26.

33. Ibid., 27.

34. Michel Foucault, *Madness and Civilization,* trans. Richard Howard (New York: Vintage, 1973), 11.

35. Ibid., 13.

36. See, for instance, Louis Hartz, *The Liberal Tradition in America* (New York: Harcourt Brace Jovanovich, 1955). For a discussion of Hartz, see Thomas L. Dumm, *united states* (Ithaca, NY: Cornell University Press, 1994), 15-6.

37. Foucault, *The Order of Things,* xviii.

38. For some, it might seem paradoxical to suggest that the utopian needs resistance, but such a view ignores the history of utopian thinking. For an argument that is suggestive of the one I am making here and that unfolds in regard to Tocqueville rather than Foucault, see George Kateb, *Utopia and Its Enemies* (New York: Free Press, 1963), 229-34.

39. As an exception, see George Kateb, *The Inner Ocean: Individualism and Democratic Culture* (Ithaca, NY: Cornell University Press, 1992), 136-9. Kateb, like Nietzsche (and like Foucault), seeks to reclaim a positive consequence emerging out the death of God, even though he does not minimize the event's nihilistic consequences.

40. The essay referred to here is "A Preface to Transgression," in Michel Foucault, *Language, Counter-Memory, Practice* (Ithaca, NY: Cornell University Press, 1977), 33-4.

41. Ibid., 36.

42. Ibid., 35.

43. Ibid.

44. Ibid., 35-6.

45. The limit is also the concern of deconstruction. For a study of deconstruction as a philosophy of the limit, see Drucilla Cornell, *The Philosophy of the Limit* (New York: Routledge, 1992).

46. Ibid., 37-8.

47. Berlin, "Two Concepts of Liberty," 121.

48. Ibid., 121-2.

49. Ibid., 124.

50. Ibid., 126.

51. In suggesting this, I am paralleling an argument developed by Jacques Derrida in his essay "White Mythology: Metaphor in the Text of Philosophy," trans. Alan Bass, in Jacques Derrida, *Margins of Philosophy* (Chicago: University of Chicago Press, 1982, especially Chapter 1), and elaborated on by Mark Wigley, *The Architecture of Deconstruction: Derrida's Haunt* (Cambridge: MIT Press, 1993), 207-231.

52. Wigley, *The Architecture of Deconstruction,* 18-9.

53. Berlin, "Two Concepts of Liberty," 123.

54. Ibid., 124.

55. Berlin might be said to move this question to the discussion of positive freedom, in that he sees the category of positive freedom coming close to containing within its space the conditions of the production and appropriation of space, or what could be said to be the activity through which neutral space can be imagined. But perhaps I am engaging in too creative a reconstruction here.

56. Berlin, "Two Concepts of Liberty," 125-6.

57. Ibid., 129.

58. An excellent recent discussion of how the formation of agents informs the liberal-communitarian debate is Bonnie Honig, *Political Theory and the Displacement of Politics* (Ithaca, NY: Cornell University Press, 1993), esp. chaps. 5 ("Rawls and the Remainders of Politics") and 6 ("Sandel and the Proliferation of Political Subjects"). I draw on Honig's insight regarding Rawls especially, and more generally see connections between her argument concerning *displacement* and the argument I am making concerning the struggle concerning the production of space.

A study by a liberal who has become a communitarian is conveniently, if unintentionally, provided by William Galston, a political theorist who at the time of this writing serves as an advisor to President Bill Clinton. See his *Liberal Purposes* (Cambridge: Cambridge University Press, 1991).

59. Honig, *Political Theory,* 164.

60. Berlin, "Two Concepts of Liberty," 131.

61. Ibid., 134.

62. Ibid., 145, 151.

63. Ibid., 148.

64. Ibid., 154.

65. Ibid., 155, 158. Charles Taylor seeks to expand on this insight in his essay *Multiculturalism and "The Politics of Recognition,"* with commentaries by Amy Gutmann, ed., Steven Rockefeller, Michael Walzer, and Susan Wolf (Princeton, NJ: Princeton University Press, 1992). For a critical response to this essay, see Thomas L. Dumm, "Liberalism and Strangers," in *Political Theory* 22, no. 1 (February 1994).

66. Berlin, "Two Concepts of Liberty," 160.

67. Ibid., 160.

68. Ibid., 163.

69. Ibid.

70. Ibid., 165.

71. Ibid., 166.

72. Ibid., 167.
73. Ibid., 165-6.
74. Berlin writes commonsensically of the normal:

When I speak of being normal, part of what I mean is that a person could not break these rules easily, without a qualm of revulsion. It is such rules as these that are broken when a man is declared guilty without trial, or punished under retroactive law; when children are ordered to denounce their parents, friends to betray one another, soldiers to use methods of barbarism; when men are tortured or murdered, or minorities are massacred because they irritate a majority or a tyrant. Such acts, even if they are made legal by the sovereign, cause horror even in these days, and this springs from the recognition of the moral validity—irrespective of the laws—of some absolute barriers to the imposition of one man's will on another. (p. 166)

These examples, however, evade the question of how the normal operates as a form of power. As I elaborate on later (esp. in Chapter 4), for Foucault, normalization is a major force that functions to allow sovereignty to operate under the cover of rights.

75. Ibid., 171.
76. Ibid., 172.
77. This theme is developed more fully by Judith Shklar in her "The Liberalism of Fear," in Nancy Rosenblum, ed., *Liberalism and the Moral Life* (Cambridge, MA: Harvard University Press, 1989), 21-38.
78. Berlin appeals to the "normal" in the concluding paragraph of an essay in which one would not expect (or at least, I did not expect) to find him do so, and thus he undermines his strongest case against the dead hand of historical understanding. In his essay "Historical Inevitability," resisting the idea of succumbing to "irresistible" forces of history that will somehow set things right or operate above the threshold of their experience, he writes the following:

And in the course of this they [historical determinists] describe the normal lives lived by men in terms which fail to mark the most important psychological and moral distinctions known to us. This they do in the service of an imaginary science; and, like the astrologers and soothsayers whom they have succeeded, cast up their eyes to the clouds, and speak in immense, unsubstantiated images and similes, in deeply misleading metaphors and allegories, and make use of hypnotic formulae with little regard for experience, or rational argument, or tests of proven reliability. (*Four Essays on Liberty,* 116)

Here Berlin resorts to the common sense of the norm, not noticing how the categories he seeks are themselves contestable and have been contested in pejorative terms that more than match his own dismissive rhetoric.

79. I am conjecturing here, although it seems to me that Foucault's attraction to the medieval period had little to do with a religious sensibility on his part but did in fact have to do with his aesthetic appreciation of how certain rites were imbued with the possibility of expressing freedom.

80. Foucault, "A Preface to Transgression," 32. It should be noted that this essay has a complicated role in Foucault's intellectual biography. It together with an essay entitled "My Body, This Paper, This Fire" (*Oxford Literary Review* 4, no. 1) are reprinted as appendices to

the second edition of *Histoire de la folie à l'âge classique* (Paris: Gallimard, 1972) and are generally understood to constitute Foucault's response to the critique of his work presented by Jacques Derrida in "Cogito and the History of Madness," *Writing and Difference,* trans. Alan Bass (Chicago: University of Chicago Press, 1978). To simplify a critique that is very complex, in its most important moments Derrida's analysis suggests that Foucault's historicization of madness does not go to the heart of the problem of the relationship of madness to reason because it does not enable Foucault to do more than perpetuate the marginalization of madness in the face of Logos. Derrida's response to the problem of logocentrism eventuates in the emergence of his pedagogy of deconstruction. Foucault's response to Derrida's critique is twofold: In "My Body, This Paper, This Fire," he suggests that to demonstrate discursive displacements of subjectivity avoids the problem from which Derrida suggests he suffers; in his turn, Foucault suggests that there is an excessive "textuality" to deconstruction. Eventually, the positions of the two moved closer together. For an overview of the debate between Foucault and Derrida, albeit one that seems to misapprehend both of their positions in regard to their respective critiques of reason and their relationships to Nietzsche and Heidegger, see Roy Boyne, *Foucault and Derrida: The Other Side of Reason* (London: Unwin & Hyman, 1990).

81. Here I am thinking of the concept of the "memory trace," developed most famously in Foucault's *Civilizations and Its Discontents,* trans. James Strachey (New York: W. W. Norton, 1989), 16-20. More generally, see his *The Interpretation of Dreams,* trans. James Strachey (New York: W. W. Norton, 1989).

82. Berlin, "Historical Inevitability," *Four Essays on Liberty,* 116.

83. I address this perhaps most famous aspect of Foucault's political thought in Chapter 3.

3

Freedom and Disciplinary Society

I wouldn't want what I may have said or written to be seen as laying any claims to totality. . . . My books aren't treatises in philosophy or studies of history: at most, they are philosophical fragments put to work in a historical field of problems.

—*L'impossible prison*

The publication of *Discipline and Punish* in 1975 represented a new moment in Foucault's thought. It is possible to mark this new development to the period of at least 1970, when he was appointed to the Collège de France. After the events of 1968, and especially from 1970 through 1975, Foucault's activism as a radical in politics intensified. The polarization of politics in France in response to the rise of new liberation movements was placing intense demands upon the intelligentsia. Upon his

Epigraph taken from "Postface" to *L'impossible prison: Recherches sur le système pénitentiaire au XIX siècle,* ed. Michelle Perrot (Paris: Seuil, 1980), 317.

return to France from Algiers, where he had been during the events of May 1968, Foucault found himself in the midst of a series of radical challenges to the political order, many initiated by students in a left (Maoist-situationist-anarchist) opposition to the French Communist Party, which had opposed the student movement during the events of May. In part as a result of this experience, Foucault became deeply concerned with the status of prisoners and was instrumental in founding an organization, Group d'Information sur les Prisons (GIP), that had as its primary purpose the transmission of information concerning the conditions of the French prison system. During this period he also was becoming more explicit in his elaboration of Nietzschean themes, especially devoting himself to thinking about how Nietzsche's ideas concerning genealogy reflect a concern with the relationship between power and knowledge. But the emergence of his thinking about Nietzsche is inflected by experience in ways that transfigure some basic Nietzschean insights.[1]

Discipline and Punish solidified Foucault's reputation as the most important French intellectual since Sartre. It also underlined the uniqueness of Foucault's political theory, one that emerges as a rigorous combination of historical erudition and a willingness to interrogate the viability of our way of being in the world.[2] *Discipline and Punish* should perhaps be called a complete book. Ironically, it has been condemned for its thoroughness, the grand sweep of its theses concerning power, and its relentless insistence on the need to consider the importance of punishment in the maintenance of modern political order. More than anything else, *Discipline and Punish* has been subject to a very unusual criticism. Many of its detractors have suggested that it offers such a complete explanation for the oppressive dimension of the present that any possibilities for authentic political responses to existing conditions are precluded by the very force of present conditions. Its theorization of power, it has been argued, is monolithic. Its introduction of Jeremy Bentham's strange architectural figure of the Panopticon and the suggestion that this figure represents an exemplar of modern power, it has been said, is obscurantist. And its proposal that we subjects of modern political orders understand ourselves as products of a series of arrangements of power, it has been claimed—especially by political theorists—is hyperbole, which, if taken seriously, could lead only to our rattling the chains of our confinement.

There are, in fact, many places in the text of *Discipline and Punish* where it seems as though Foucault is suggesting that the emergence of disciplinary society condemns humankind to a perpetual punishment. The sweeping scope of disciplinary society, the idea of a "carceral network" that has "no outside," the complex interrelationship of power/knowledge—all of these motifs present an image of disciplinary society that is unrelenting in its totality. And it is undeniable that a major thesis presented in *Discipline and Punish* is that "the soul is the prison of the body." This thesis is reflected in the not-so-hidden irony of the book's subtitle, "The Birth of the Prison." So it hardly helps to mitigate the idea of a totalistic thesis at work when one realizes that Foucault's subtitle refers to the birth of the modern soul, a birth that can be understood as synonymous with the conditions that give rise to the modern subject. Moreover, Foucault directly suggests at different points in the book that he is describing the history of the present, the techniques through which individuals are produced and the knowledge that may be gained of them, and the way in which the body is reduced as a political force by its utilization within a system of production not merely of goods but of power itself. The idea that power might exist as the medium through which every human phenomenon might be seen only as an effect— this is, no doubt, the most excoriated idea to be found in *Discipline and Punish* (and, to the extent that my characterization is accurate, an idea that deserves to be vilified).

But as ubiquitous as the functioning of power/knowledge is in the constitution of disciplinary society for Foucault, discipline is not simply an expression of it. Foucault focuses on the complex of power/knowledge as it unfolds within a given order, locating the biases in power/knowledge in an attempt to understand what shifts and changes in that order might be possible. By the compound power/knowledge, he means to say that expressions of power are never unmediated but, instead, unfold in the various ways it is possible to know relationships of domination and force. Indeed, Foucault suggests (in an interview contemporaneous with the publication of *Discipline and Punish*) that it is precisely the problem of explaining power, not being able readily to identify it, only seeing it through its effects, that is the concern animating *Discipline and Punish* and other works.[3] For this reason, among others, *Discipline and Punish* is almost inexhaustible in its references and gestures toward systems of thought and practice through which it is possible to understand power.

Indeed, it is as a system of references that one might most properly see how *Discipline and Punish* functions as a complete book. Its fecundity is such that it can be comprehended as a rewriting of much of the social theory of the past century, or, for less generous readers, as simple cribbing from sources such readers always seem to know better. When Foucault's reputation in the United States was beginning to take off as a consequence of this book's reception, this implicitly referential character of *Discipline and Punish* had philosophers and social theorists saying as much: What's the big deal? Foucault, they were inclined to argue, is only a gloss on Emile Durkheim, or Max Weber, or the more prominent members of the Frankfurt School, or Georg Simmel, or Ernst Cassirer, or Hannah Arendt, or Thomas Kuhn, or (even) Henry David Thoreau. But the seeming uncanniness of his work is not a consequence of his lack of originality. One might better imagine Foucault as a sort of intellectual Elvis. His referentiality is not a sign of his lack of originality but is, instead, an artifact of the unusually meticulous preparation of the archival retrieval that bears the burden of his genealogy. For it is the unspoken character of genealogy as practiced by Foucault that it is an attempt to trace the character of an age through the dry and dusty documents that betray its unthought practices. In tracing those archives, genealogy brings those practices to visibility and thus makes their life more amenable to change.

The Right to Make Promises

As I have already noted, probably the most important single influence on *Discipline and Punish* is provided by the works of Nietzsche, even though there is not a single direct reference to Nietzsche in the book. One way to decipher *Discipline and Punish* is as a subtle dialogue with Nietzsche concerning the fate of modernity. The book's subtitle, "The Birth of the Prison," not only refers to the genealogy of the modern soul, it also is an ironic gesture made in the direction of Nietzsche's first book, *The Birth of Tragedy*. A reader might pause over the connections between Foucault and Nietzsche in this book because even in the title Foucault's study of discipline is marked by his debt to important elements of Nietzsche's philosophy. One might, for instance, notice that in a preface written upon the reissuance of *The Birth of Tragedy*, Nietzsche suggests that the concern animating his investigation into the Apollonian and Dionysian is what is most important, not the book itself, which was, as he put it, constructed of "overgreen" personal experiences.[4] That concern was expressed most simply in one of many questions that Nietzsche advanced in his introduction to *The Birth of Tragedy*'s second edition: "Is there a pessimism of strength?" For Nietzsche, the possibility that there is such a pessimism is indicated not least by the weakness implicit in Socrates' all too successful escape from its effects through the ruse of the dialectic. "Is the resolve to be so scientific about everything perhaps a kind of fear of, an escape from, pessimism? A subtle last resort against—*truth*?"[5]

The question of truth was frightful and dangerous for the young Nietzsche to ask, as he himself appreciated. Foucault is also deeply aware of the dangerous implications of the question. And the truth he seeks in *Discipline and Punish* can only be revealed through an interrogation of practices, an interrogation that places the sciences of the human, especially the social sciences, into question in such a way as to allow us to move toward their truth. Foucault asks that all of us who are concerned with the practice of freedom pause before the question of truth because it bears so directly upon freedom's fate. *Discipline and Punish* is dedicated to tracing the rituals of truth that shape the possibilities of our being free. Because of his sensitivity to Nietzsche he recognizes that the question of truth opens up the question of perspectivism. Perspectivism introduces us to the paradox initiating Nietzsche's concern about the will to power: perspectivism thus contains a core truth about the era in which we live. It might be important to ask, then, how might one begin to think about the operations of the will to power in relationship to our present? How does such a will inform the constitution of truth in our time?

We might note that in referring the question of truth to what he was to call "the history of the present," Foucault makes Nietzsche's question more widely available than it has been made before. "What is our truth?" is the most important question informing the structure and substance of *Discipline and Punish*. Moreover, in contradistinction to Nietzsche, Foucault wants that question to be asked by ordinary citizens as well as critical intellectuals. His book is intended for a wide audience by design. As he said in an interview, "I know that people concerned with the prisons, lawyers, educators, prison visitors, not to mention the prisoners themselves, have read it; and it was precisely such people I was addressing to begin with."[6] Although it would be an exaggeration to claim that *Discipline and Punish* is an easy book to read and understand, nonetheless, in that book and in his exhaustive efforts to explain it, Foucault probably does more to democratize the Nietzschean insight into the problem of modernity than anyone else, with consequences that cannot yet be fully assessed.[7] In opening up the Nietzschean problematic to wide discussion, Foucault moves directly against the force of Nietzsche's overt, if heavily qualified, political claims for an aristocratic politics. Foucault is more concerned to seek the widespread engagement of those who have been marginalized by the normalizing forces of the modern era.

The relationship of *Discipline and Punish* to Nietzsche's work is probably most direct in the way Foucault imitates, deepens, and transforms the argument advanced in the second essay of Nietzsche's *On the Genealogy of Morals*, "On 'Guilt,' 'Bad Conscience,' and the Like."[8] The distinctive argument advanced by Nietzsche in that essay concerns the role of pain in the creation of memory. The manipulation of pain through torture lies at the core of the development of the sense of indebtedness, a basic element in the system of exchange that Nietzsche identifies as the heart of guilt. The inquiry into such a complicated yet essential matter is summarized in an amazing question with which Nietzsche initiates his inquiry: "To breed an animal *with the right to make promises*—is this not the paradoxical task that nature has set itself in the case of man? is it not the real problem regarding man?"[9] Why does this question represent the "real" problem concerning man? For Nietzsche, understanding the elevation of humans above their animal being is a necessary prerequisite to understanding how we are to overcome ourselves now.

Nietzsche understood the human being to be a forgetful animal who must overcome forgetfulness to realize his nature. To begin to understand the process of how we overcome our forgetfulness and come to be an animal with the right to make promises, Nietzsche found it necessary to describe the first "task" of humans as that of willing into existence a memory to will. This task is paradoxical, perhaps the most paradoxical task of all. Indeed, Nietzsche presents us with a problem that in the end is one of practice: how are humans to develop techniques of remembering that will be remembered long enough so that we will not forget? To make active one's desire for anything is to project oneself into the future, and to do that one must come to have a past to remember. And yet, in the absence of memory, there is no past to remember. This is the raison d'être of pain. Through practices of repetitive pain, the beating into the body of a few basic prohibitions, humans will learn to remember. Thus, the very first act of will is that of willing memory so that one can remember future intentions. And the first memory will be a memory of pain.

It might be said that we are pained into being. Moreover, pain is something we can give to each other, a first gift. The deliberate, intentional, all too human infliction of pain, punishment in its most general sense, torture specifically, thus looms large in Nietzsche's genealogy of guilt. In adopting a perspective that allows for putting punishment first among the qualities by which we become human, Nietzsche and those who have followed in his path have worked to reestablish an ambiguous truth from the *Book of Job,* a book that ends in an ambiguous acceptance of the mortality of human being. Job ends his confrontation with God by stating simply, "I will be quiet, comforted that I am dust."[10] This very early anticipation of elements of stoicism is not in tune with the utopian strains that have marked the modern age and that emerge from a tradition in which God is created in an image of asceticism. Putting punishment first radically revises the image of God. Putting punishment first means taking seriously the fact that as sentient beings we are pained into existence, not fallen from a higher plane of being, and not destined to recover a pristine state of grace. But the controversies that arise from following the implications of that fact are astonishing in scope and depth.[11]

Nietzsche discusses at length how memory is only inscribed after long suffering. The achievement of a being who could be counted on required much training. "Man himself," he writes, "must first of all have to become *calculable, regular, necessary,* even in his own image of himself, if he is able to stand securely for *his own future,* which is what he who promises does!"[12] Thus, in his brief survey of the ways in which we are pained into memory, Nietzsche provides an inspiration for the way Foucault begins *Discipline and Punish.* Nietzsche writes, "Man could never do without blood, torture, and sacrifices when he felt the need to create a memory for himself."[13] Human sacrifice, ritual castration, drawing and quartering, flaying—all play a role in the cruelty underlying morality, the five or six "I will nots" to which he sardonically refers. But Nietzsche goes further. If cruelty lies at the heart of our good things, he asks, why do we so little note it? It is at this point that the concept of guilt, its relationship to debt, and the relationship of both to sovereignty come into play. In the relationship of guilt to debt Nietzsche uncovers some of the subterranean forces that make individuals sovereign bearers of the right to promise. He does so by focusing attention on the origins of a common legal relationship, that of the contract, which for Nietzsche in essence is also the origin of guilt. The debtor in a contract was able to *promise* precisely because *what* was promised at bottom was a pledge of replacing what he owed with a more basic possession—his body.[14] The original "logic of compensation," Nietzsche claims, suggests that the creditor ultimately would be able to put into place the pleasure of enacting a cruelty upon the debtor's body as compensation for whatever else he might be owed.

This structure of compensation is at the core of modern criminal punishment, in which any attempt to sentence someone must fall upon the scale of the incommensurability of just deserts. This structure also frames guilt in terms that are always necessarily associated with debt and a need to balance the books. But this structure is also open-ended in a variety of ways. In mundane life, the ultimate call for the pound of flesh is rarely made (although it is also a truism that the pound of flesh is eventually extracted one way or another over the course of a life). More important, not only is there no conclusion to the compensatory displacements of debt, there is also no conclusion to the pain that initiates the debt relationship because all attempts to collect debts become implicated in new cruelties. Cruelty is not pain but a relationship between people forged through the infliction of pain, a relationship that is itself not determined in a final, definitive direction.[15] We might see Foucault's task in *Discipline and Punish* as being to open up the structure of cruelty in all of its complexity. He seeks to show how the moral order of the modern age operates through mechanisms that cannot be dissociated from cruelty so that we might know better how to comprehend the structures of power that we inhabit and that shape our consciences.

Nietzsche's argument concerning the relationship of guilt to debt has been dismissed or ignored by many liberal theorists (or absorbed and normalized by the [lesser] followers of Freud). And yet it has never been refuted, only denied, ignored, or tamed by being reduced to a purely interior phenomenon. To paraphrase Nietzsche, our modern philosophers have too often sided with Kant, pretending that the categorical imperative does *not* smell of cruelty. At their best, such moralists have concentrated on Nietzsche's suggestions concerning the ways in which the will to remember contributes to what he was to call "the *internalization* of man."[16]

But even in psychoanalysis the study of *ressentiment* rarely leads to a practice of the arts of the self. Much more often, and to the detriment of psychoanalysis, it leads to a more common therapeutic avoidance of the unsettling truths concerning the ubiquitous quality of cruelty in the constitution of life.

Suppose we ask this question: Cruelty is always punishing, but is it punishment?[17] Cruelty is punishment to the extent that punishment remains corporal because the infliction of punishment always contains an element of bodily pain. The corporeality of punishment is insisted upon by Foucault, even as it apparently becomes most attenuated, because, like Nietzsche, Foucault insists that agency is constituted through the memory of pain. In fact, for Foucault it is less the internalization of man, the creation of depth, bad conscience, and the like—in short, all the elements that concern the logic of promises—that must be comprehended in order to study adequately disciplinary society. He understands Nietzsche to have accomplished much of this task already. Foucault focuses instead on another anchor of Nietzsche's question concerning the paradoxical task of making an animal with the right to make promises. This question of *right* concerns Foucault because while the structure of a promise depends upon memory and memory depends upon an infliction of cruelty, the issuance of a right emerges from another element of this sovereign power. This other element of sovereign power lies in the space of whatever we might call our freedom. Freedom itself depends less upon the practices of memory than upon the construction of the spaces enabled by those practices. For Foucault freedom is a practice, which in a given regime of truth depends upon those relationships that it is possible to cultivate at the intersection of the varying institutional forms that shape power/knowledge.

"The right to make promises" is a phrase that condenses and shows the intimacy of the relationship that obtains between the two concepts of liberty that Isaiah Berlin attempts to keep separate.[18] The internalization that Berlin associated with positive liberty—the promising or commitment of self that precedes binding and that is the condition of that further, interagential relationship that is the presupposition of political obligations—is necessarily a right because its exercise is the expression of how, fundamentally or ontologically, we are free, free in reference to our exercise of freedom. This understanding of the secondhand character of freedom is perhaps the most fundamental way in which Nietzsche's view can be distinguished from that of Kant and other "deontological" liberals. When Nietzsche suggests that the categorical imperative "smells of cruelty,"[19] he is referring to that which must be forgotten in order for the practice of a morality that pretends to be innocent to proceed. That species of forgetfulness is not admired by Nietzsche because he understands it as a false forgetting, a denial of the memory established through much pain and suffering, so that one can continue to suffer in the name of something supposedly better than oneself.

For Foucault, this "other debt" to Nietzsche, that which concerns his unveiling of the importance of the right to make promises and how it concerns the practices of freedom, is quietly and profoundly discharged in *Discipline and Punish*. Foucault pays homage to Nietzsche in more ways than simply following Nietzsche's agenda. He does so by rethinking the political implications of Nietzsche's insight, both by opening vision to a new array of possibilities and by closing off the possibility that the terms of any new truth might be worked through without first coming to terms with the difficult pain of understanding our ways of being cruel to each other. In short, in *Discipline and Punish* Foucault defines the practical conditions through which modern freedom came into being. He was able to do so by remembering precisely that fact which the force of modern disciplinary society has made too easy to forget—the fact of embodiment, the fact that the body is always what is at issue. The focus on cruelty becomes a way of prying open certain prejudices concerning the status of the body as an unproblematic receptacle of rights. For Foucault, following Nietzsche, the body is prepared by the pain it suffers.

Discipline and Punish is at root a book about the practices of freedom and the conditions that bear upon those practices in the modern era. If we approach this book with this idea in mind, we might come to understand *Discipline and Punish* as a preparatory text, a book that sets an agenda for uncovering not only the terms of our imprisonment but the conditions of our freedom. It is Foucault's conviction that only if one meets the demand of understanding how we are pained into being, refusing to shirk from this paradoxical truth of our existence, might it be possible to appreciate our political way of thinking in its most horrific implications and begin to rethink our relationship to truth. In this sense, Foucault sets a formidable agenda for those who would seek to think differently about the range of political possibilities available to us at this juncture in the history of human being.

Yet even this insight concerning the paradoxes of freedom does not exhaust Foucault's contribution to its study. If we decide that it is irresponsible simply to condemn cruelty, there are still different ways in which we might come to understand its ineradicable role in the constitution of morality. If Foucault were "only" a latter-day Bataille or Marquis de Sade, he could not claim even the same attention as his (too often misunderstood) predecessors. But Foucault is not only, or even primarily, a student of cruelty. Although his work is anchored in a deep appreciation of the role that cruelty plays in the emergence of promising, as I have already tried to emphasize, Foucault is as concerned with and every bit as appreciative of the role that freedom plays in the emergence of the multiplicity of rights through which the modern repertoire of political arrangements might be broadened. His arguments concerning the production of space and the human capacity to establish transgressions of space incite us to know freedom not merely as a name but as a set of practices through which we might better know how we are free. Indeed, the outlines of how we are free inform the basic structure of his theory of discipline.

A combination of an arcane erudition in the arts that shape the spatialization of modern experience and a profoundly felt pain that comes with knowledge of the extent of the confinements of modern experience, confinements that mark a futile (and cruel) attempt to evade the cruelties of human being, decisively mark Foucault's thought as he works through the genealogy of the modern soul. It turns out to be the case that the modern capacity to punish is the modern capacity to be human. Studying this style of punishment, discipline, in its complexity allows us to better understand how we might be free, by enabling us to know how freedom depends upon the painful constitution of the spaces through which it is exercised.

Migrations of the Sovereign Body

The opening pages of *Discipline and Punish* contain a famous juxtaposition of two descriptions: the first, the execution of Damien the regicide by drawing and quartering, a bloody, extremely cruel, and explicitly disturbing event, rendered by Foucault with documentary immediacy; the other, a prison timetable from some seventy years later, dry and dusty, precise and totally uneventful. The drama of the comparison is immediate, power-ful, and so often noted by commentators as to have become a bit of a cliché. It usefully contrasts a punishment that operates as display with one that displaces display with the normalizing judgment that Foucault describes in detail in his analysis of discipline. This beginning contains the core elements of the narrative Foucault presents: this movement, so sudden and yet so glacially subtle, is a trace of the power that will confine the tortured body within the modern soul. We learn that the calm order of the modern is itself a dead end, the death of the body in the name of bureaucratic order. The archive of pain is replaced with the archive of habit, and we are in our familiar world containing all of the modern forms of organization and paperwork. This beginning might tell us that we are caught in this world, that our days will be composed of our regular schedules: rising, eating, working, praying, and sleeping.

Perhaps too much attention has focused on this beginning, attention that obscures the complexity of the argument that follows. That is precisely why it may be useful to focus on another beginning. This other beginning occurs when Foucault poses a question that seems, on first reading, to be easily answerable. "What would a non-corporal punishment be?" he asks.[20] This question can be responded to immediately by pointing to confinement, parole, probation, fines, chastisement, or any one of a series of sanctions that does not implicate the human body in immediate, physical pain. These sanctions, which only incidentally and forgettably touch upon bodies, seem to work to underscore the abstract, internal character of modern punish-ment. We seek to bypass bodies and focus on souls in our desire to create a punishment that will dignify our modern selves. The great reforms that eliminated legal torture and operated to rehabilitate were designed to punish without touching bodies. Or were they?

Well aware of the arguments of reformers, Foucault poses this question concerning the (non)corporal character of punishment after a very quick and sweeping survey of the trajectory that punishment followed in the years after it turned inward from being a spectacle, that is, during that interval between the decline of the European monarchy and the rise of republican regimes when punishment became the most hidden part of the legitimate functioning of governments. Through a series of technological mutations, the body becomes an instrument of punishment, no longer its end, its object. Justice would no longer glorify its strength by marking the body.

Indeed, conviction itself is to mark the offender with shame. In keeping with the new morality of punishment, new techniques of execution were introduced—the hanging machine, the guillotine. These devices eventually focused attention upon the moment of death in the most dramatic punishment of all, capital punishment, reducing the act that had once been an extended and microcosmic infinity of pain to a single blow, an event over with in a split second. As Foucault suggests, "The guillotine takes life almost without touching the body, just as prison deprives of liberty or a fine reduces wealth."[21]

But throughout this discussion of the reduction of spectacle and the prohibition of torture, and transformations that occurred in punishment as the result, Foucault hesitates to cross a threshold. He will not pretend, as, for instance, someone like Jean Baudrillard would pretend, that we might somehow let the body disappear, as if one could enact a punishment that would totally eliminate the body either as object *or* as medium without also eliminating everything else in life.[22] In every mechanism of the criminal justice designed to replace that of the *supplice,* Foucault suggests "there remains a trace of 'torture' . . . a trace that has not been entirely overcome, but which is enveloped, increasingly, by the non-corporal nature of the penal system."[23] The imprisonment of the body thus does not imply that the body becomes irrelevant, or that it is paralyzed, but instead that it enters into a new modality in relationship to political power. The body, in the newer regime, is to become an object of political power by becoming regularized, constrained, and normalized. It is to become a part of a great ensemble of mechanisms, put into the service of a particular regime that Foucault is to name disciplinary society.

What is this body that is to be put to such a use? Or rather, what *was* it? (The bodies we inhabit—can we really say that they *are* essentially the same as those subjected to earlier cruelties? And this possibility, of a radical historicity informing bodily existence itself, not merely the appellation "man" that we give it, that signifies the values of a particular civilization, is this not the most disturbing question of all, this question that Nietzsche brought forth for our consideration, this question that has almost been lost in its vulgarization, in its shoddy appropriation by the latter-day eugenicists of our century, and in its popularization via demonology by those lazy moralists who are dull enough simply to accept the fascist reading of Nietzsche?) It may be that the bodies we inhabit have been subjected to and are shaped by a more sophisticated mnemonics of pain than could ever be possible in the earlier regime of torture and, consequentially, are now associated with the subtle forces that conjoin any assertion of an abstract set of rights. A simple summary suggests that from a singular focus on the pain that would be effected by the torturer, which was intrinsic to the old regime of truth, and was composed of a knowledge of offense, offender, and law, the new regime of truth was to ask other questions and seek other results. What is this act that has been committed? To what field of reality does it properly belong? What caused the offender to do what he did? Even as such questions are asked, the number of points at which judgments occur multiplies, and the act of judgment itself is stripped of its grandeur and finality. Judgment comes to be blended with other functions. "A whole set of assessing, diagnostic, prognostic, normative judgments concerning the criminal have become lodged in the framework of penal judgment."[24] Judges find that they are judging much more than crimes. In the process of sentencing, they do something other than judging altogether. And finally, they do not judge alone; they are joined by a multitude of experts.[25]

These transformations in the way in which criminals are punished have long been noted by those who have studied the history of crime, and by those who call themselves criminologists, but they are evidence as well of a shift in how the bodies of those subjected to judgment are invested in power relations. To uncover that shift it is necessary "to study the metamorphosis of punitive methods on the basis of a political technology of the body in which might be read a common history of power relations and object relations."[26] In doing so, one will need to think through a particular political economy of the body, one perhaps not indebted to Freud but certainly one that parallels Freud's understanding of how there might be an economy of psychic pain and pleasure.[27] For Foucault, as opposed to Freud, the economy of pain and pleasure is not closed, the body itself is potentially open to a greater energy via the power of imagination than it is in the (surprisingly variable) closed economy that Freud developed.

This presumption of a malleability of the body is a result of Foucault's appreciation of the relationship between the materiality of the body and its symbolic role in the politics of sovereignty. The attention he pays early in *Discipline and Punish* to the medieval theological concept of the King's two bodies is intended to illuminate the role of the body in the development of political imagination. The King's body was a double body, composed of two elements, since it involved "not only the transitory element that is born and dies, but another that remains unchanged by time and is maintained as the physical yet intangible support of the kingdom."[28] This duality is at the center of a complex set of power relationships. Around it "are organized an iconography, a political theory of monarchy, legal mechanisms that distinguish between as well as link the person of the King and the demands of the Crown, and a whole ritual that reaches its height in the coronation, the funeral and the ceremonies of submission."[29] The King's body was sovereign, and around the disintegration of the King's sovereignty (and body) a new form of right and a new mode of power would emerge. At this peculiar moment in Foucault's text, in the conclusion of the introduction, Foucault asks the reader to imagine the majesty of the King's body having as its double what he referred to as "the least body of the condemned man," a person who calls forth his own theoretical discourse, one who is "the symmetrical, inverted figure of the king."[30]

This subjected body gives rise to the modern soul; it is the product of its own reality, a result of "a functioning of power on those who are punished."[31] Foucault's focus on the creation of this soul enables him to show, from a point of view radically within the operations of power, a profound transformation in the meaning of sovereignty from the medieval to the modern era. What happens to the body of the least condemned man has its inverted parallel in what happens to the King's body. Foucault realizes his project by concentrating his attention on the dispersal of the King's sovereignty, a movement in which the power of the King's body is to be redistributed to—and inside of—modern subjects. In turn, by tracing this dispersal of sovereign powers he is able to illuminate what we might call the interiority of power relations, shedding light on them from out-side.[32] This illumination is the project of "a correlative history of the modern soul and of a new power to judge: a genealogy of the present scientifico-legal complex from which the power to punish derives its bases, justifications and rules, from which it extends its effects and by which it masks its exorbitant singularity."[33]

Much remains unsaid in such a summary: the rules that Foucault suggests one follow as one engages in such a study, for instance, or the purpose of an overt reliance upon the shock value of a detailed recitation of torturous death. But at issue in the birth of the soul, the birth of the prison, is not how cruel humans are. Such a question has been asked and answered by Nietzsche.

We might better advance our thinking if we try to ask *how humans are cruel,* what range of cruelties may have been enacted, how such cruelties have interacted with other elements of life, and what the consequences for the value of life the presence of an element of cruelty may have. As a result, the questions we might then ask of each other concerning our political projects are of a different sort: What modes of power will operate? What changes in the meaning of sovereignty will attend its migration from king to agent? What forms of production will be associated with this shift, and what will it mean to be human when the modality of cruelty shifts, and the body, even as it disappears from view, becomes the site of more intensive struggles than it has before?

The migration of sovereignty is the name we might give to the gravitation of the characteristics of a representative power from the external order of positive freedom to the internal subjectivity that makes up the ground of the agent who bears rights, an agent who is to be given freedom as a gift of the order within which he or she exists. Sovereignty itself presents freedom as a habitation of power, as the demonstration of an ability of sovereignty to command and restrain. This force of sovereignty is itself a name we give to the principle of command, to the order that establishes possible ways of being in the world. For Foucault, the question concerning sovereignty is whether its own being can be called into question or whether, instead, it has so closely become identified with a will to power that it must remain unthought. To provide an answer to this question, Foucault traces the operations of sovereign power as they shift from the King's two bodies to the body of the modern subject. The communicating link between the two is the pain suffered by modern subjects for the crimes that they commit against the sovereign order itself. But it turns out that the answer opens up yet another complexity, one that can be summarized in another deceptively simple question: What is a crime? In the discussion of sovereignty and power, of condemnation and punishment, of the body and soul, that which is fundamental to all of these phenomena, a common factor that seems to link them, to define them by establishing the limits of their meanings and the terms of their transgressions, is crime itself. Is there a pure crime, or, as an alternative, a pure criminality, to which we might refer? Again we must ask: What is a crime?

Foucault's answer is this: A crime is what is punished.

With this answer Foucault refuses the conventions of liberal justice that have been used to claim that a crime is what violates a law. This need, it turns out, is part of a forgetfulness that allows the order to pretend to be immutable, protecting inviolable beings. Foucault's investigation into the rituals of punishment is intended to show how the history of all common laws is connected to the redirection of the force of punishment. When the law was the word of the sovereign enforced by the sword,[34] the reasonableness of law was derived from the power of the King and the faith that people had in the King's divine right. The establishment of modern, conventional, positive law supplanted this arbitrary character of law, but with what? The core principle of "rule of law" places law itself in the position of the king.

Although many modern jurists have interpreted the decline of monarchy and the rise of regimes based upon rights as a sign of the decline of the rule of sovereignty, and the partial displacement of the power of sovereignty that accompanies the decline of its rule with a rise in the rights of individuals, for Foucault the matter is much more complicated. Sovereignty, indeed the sovereignty that still depends upon an imagined King, persists as the mode through which rights are known and exercised, even as the transformation of punishment results in a decline of the exercise of sovereign power and the rise of another—disciplinary power—linked to but dramatically different from sovereign right. But to understand how the power of discipline was to come into being, we would need to follow a course of thought that goes against the grain of the way the power of sovereignty is conventionally understood. Sovereignty is typically seen now as a *principle* rather than a force, and it no longer is perceived as inhering in any material body.

In a lecture on the progress of his work in tracing this "disappearance" of sovereign right, Foucault discusses the path one might follow if one is to think about discipline's role as a mode of power. He advances his discussion by comparing his thoughts about sovereign power to Hobbes's great project in *Leviathan.*

Insofar as he is a fabricated man, Leviathan is no other than the amalgamation of a certain number of separate individualities, who find themselves reunited by the complex of elements that go to compose the State; but at the heart of the State, or rather, at its head, there exists something which constitutes it as such, and this is sovereignty, which Hobbes says is precisely the spirit of Leviathan. Well, rather than worry about the problem of the central spirit, I believe that we must attempt to study the myriad of bodies which are constituted as peripheral *subjects* as a result of the effects of power.[35]

Studying those bodies means eschewing "the model of the Leviathan in the study of power," but for Foucault it does not at all mean that sovereignty ceases to exist or that rights disappear. Instead, he argues,

Modern society . . . has been characterized on the one hand, by a legislation, a discourse, an organization based on public right, whose principle of articulation is the social body and the delegative status of each citizen; and on the other hand, by a closely linked grid of disciplinary coercions whose purpose is in fact to assure the cohesion of this same social body. Though a theory of right is a necessary companion to this grid, it cannot in any event provide the terms of its endorsement. Hence these two limits, a right of sovereignty and a mechanism of discipline, which define, I believe, the arena in which power is exercised. But these two limits are so heterogeneous that they cannot possibly be reduced to each other. The powers of modern society are exercised through, on the basis of, and by virtue of this very heterogeneity between a public right of sovereignty and a polymorphous disciplinary mechanism.[36]

Here Foucault provides the core of an analysis of the relationship among sovereignty, rights, and discipline. He focuses on the spatial elements of this relationship to cast greater light on how the exercise of power is deeply connected to the organization of what can be known. There are two separate spaces, one defined by the reciprocal boundaries of sovereignty and right, and one defined by discipline. These spaces are incommensurately organized and yet are connected through a common posture imposed upon the bodies that are exercised in their parallel domains. Bodies themselves form the transgressive link between these heterotopias; bodies themselves constitute the sites where there occurs a strategic displacement of sovereignty from the immaterial corporeality of the King to the more general circulation in society.

The shift in the weight of justice from the self-contained power of the sovereign to the realm of public law has the ironic effect of separating the concerns of justice from the concerns of everyday life. This separation is a catalyst for the development of disciplinary society. It also gives license to those who sit in judgment to place responsibility for cruelty on those who are most likely to suffer the consequences of being caught out, of committing a cruel act that is deemed illegal by those in positions of domination. Cruelty becomes an indicator of a lack of liberality precisely because and to the extent that it is segregated from the remainder of life.[37] But this segregation works only to the extent that we are able to accept the fiction that the body does not serve as this communicating link between the orders of sovereignty and right and discipline, only to the extent that we are able to pretend that there can be such a thing as a noncorporal punishment.

The development of mechanisms through which people might be trained *not* to be caught in acts of cruelty (which still are attached to them, which still operate to define them), that is, the development of a discipline through which they might learn to behave themselves, is the other anchor of this dual spatial arrangement. ("Behaving oneself" might be understood in the fullness of its etymological associations, as an acute consciousness of self associated with the realization that one possesses oneself as an object.[38]) But disciplinary order operates as an infraspace, in tension with the organization of the space of sovereignty and rights. This tension reflects the fact that justice will operate in the interest of some more than others. But it also suggests that a simple division between those who rule and those who are ruled is impossible. Indeed, it may also mean that the political truth of our time is to be found in the imagination of a differently configured space rather than in the development of a new theory or practice of justice. Thus, for Foucault to claim that a crime is what is punished is to make explicit what is implied by the distribution and organization of the myriad bodies on the periphery of the political center and thus to shed a different light on the investments of power that might be made in the body of the condemned. The old legal rituals, which established methods for determining whether a crime had been committed, contained within them not only a method for revealing a specific truth but for establishing, through repetition, the meaning of a crime within the entire political order. Foucault's concern for the *supplice,* the judicial torture that attended the process of seeking a confession from a suspected crime-doer, unfolds into an examination of the decline of an entire political order, which is to say, an entire realm of truth. Foucault traces the organization of this ritual of the *supplice* because in doing so he hopes to trace its role in our current organization of truth.

The purpose of judicial torture was to uncover the truth of crime through the calculated and regulated production of pain. This pain was calculated through a series of conventionalized measurements. The inventiveness of medieval torture devices, the precision of such instruments as the wheel, the iron maiden, and the rack—all of this was a result of a subtle attention to the fine calibrations that might be made regarding degrees of pain that (in principle) could be extended to the moment of death. A sort of Zeno's paradox was imposed upon what might be thought of as the infinite duration of pain. In part because of this appreciation of the inventiveness with which pain might be imposed, but primarily because pain was to be put in the service of a juridical end, it was regulated through a legal code which would specify the extent and limits of the use of torture. The combination of calculation and regulation was given its expression in a liturgy of punishment that was intended both to mark the body and to provide a spectacle, thus illustrating the victorious power of the sovereign over the person who dared oppose the King's will. The liturgy of punishment was to inscribe the truth of crime both upon the body of the condemned person and in the imaginations of the other subjects of the King.

To do so, judicial torture needed to follow a careful and rigorous logic of proofs that set apart the truth of crime from the truth of everyday life. Particularly, the investigations of jurists were designed to culminate in a confession on the part of the accused. This confession was to be separated from ordinary truth by the secrecy with which it was initiated and by the public self-condemnation that would mark its culmination. The use of these elements by those seeking the truth of the crime was designed to heighten its distance from the quotidian elements of life.

This gap created by the division between secrecy and publicity was closed by the infliction of pain upon the body of the criminal. Bodily pain communicated the meaning of crime to the judge, the criminal, and the subjects of the King. Pain linked everyone, but everyone needed to be assured of the meaning conveyed by it. There was a dual process at work. Confession was taken under oath. It was also taken under the duress of torture. For Foucault, the twin elements of oath and torture resulted in a double ambiguity concerning the confession: it sought the strong proof of a "voluntary" statement of guilt on the part of the accused, yet the truth of the confession rested upon its coerced quality. Although this system was strictly regulated, it was not one of excess. Torture was an important element in a highly developed semiotic of truth, an element in the search for justice, but it was not the end of the process.

Under the regime of the *supplice,* truth was to be tortured. Truth was uncovered after an ordeal of lengthy questioning under the duress of inflicted pain. But the core truth unveiled by the confession necessarily admitted of the complexity of guilt, its degrees and ambiguities. It demonstrated how the worlds of the King and the subject were connected through the body of the tortured, confessing criminal. It suggested how those two worlds were as one. And, as if this were not enough communication, the body of the accused linked the secret investigation of the judicial tribunal to the ritual of confession and public spectacle across one other, final gap, that of temporality. Because once the confession was achieved, the spectacle of torture continued in the penalty phase. This pain, its creation and its juxtaposition to other elements of ritual through implementation, in the end marked the continuous concern for truth on the part of the judicial officials. The public liturgy of punishment made the condemned man the herald of his own crime. The execution of the sentence itself allowed for further confessions to be made, and the act of execution was constituted as an "entire poetics" in which the symbology of the crime was reproduced in the punishment. Finally, the moment of death afforded all spectators a glimpse of the immortal judgment of divinity. In short, from the beginning of the secret judicial torture to the execution, "the body, several times tortured, provides the synthesis of the reality of the deeds and the truth of the investigation, of the documents of the case and the statements of the criminal, of the crime and the punishment."[39]

Hence, the execution was part of a politics through which the power of sovereignty was exercised and in its exercise reinforced. In this world, the crime is not only something that affects the immediate victim of the crime: the King is a victim of the crime as well because it is his law that is violated and his absolute right that is challenged by the criminal act. A part of every punishment is designed not simply to redress the grievance of the immediate victim but to reestablish the rightful authority of the King. Indeed, the purpose of public execution was not, in the end, to restore justice but, instead, to reactivate the power of the sovereign; thus the dramatic incommensurability between the criminal act and the punishment to which it gave rise. It was "a policy of terror; to make everyone aware, through the body of the criminal, of the unrestrained presence of the sovereign."[40] This horrifying lack of symmetry between the criminal and the sovereign was an essential element of public execution. "A body effaced, reduced to dust and thrown to the winds, a body destroyed piece by piece by the infinite power of the sovereign constituted not only the ideal, but the real limit of punishment."[41] Foucault, citing Giambattista Vico, suggests that such a punishment constitutes itself as a "total poetics."[42] A regime organized around the principles of the *supplice* is one in which the power of the sovereign of necessity is highly visible in comparison to the subjects upon whom the poetical understanding of truth would be impressed.

This system engendered its own vulnerability, and this vulnerability was to be crucial to the eventual migration of sovereignty from the body of the King to the law. An important point of that vulnerability is the fact that the execution of punishment occurred as spectacle, which always contains a latent disorder threatening to break out, an always latent possibility of the loss of control by the agents of sovereign authority. The spectacle of punishment had to contain such an element of disorder because it was designed to re-create the threat that it was to eliminate.

The role of the executioner was of great importance in this regard because the executioner was the visible agent of the King. The art of destroying the body was not a minor one. Indeed, when executioners failed in their task, they risked having the wrath of the assembled crowd turn upon them. Foucault insists that the execution was first and foremost a moment of confrontation, a symbolic war of the criminal against sovereign right, and that the executioner was, in this sense, the embodiment of the King as warrior. "The executioner not only implemented the law, he also deployed the force; he was the agent of the violence applied, in order to master it, to the violence of the crime."[43] This role was an exceedingly intimate and strange one. Although the executioner was an agent of the King, he shared in the infamy of the condemned man. And his actual power to kill was secondhand. "The sovereign power that enjoined him to kill, and which through him did kill, was not present in him; it was not identified with his own ruthlessness."[44] Yet although the executioner was warrior, the other head of the King, as the font of justice, was not given over to him. The great responsibility that rested in the hands of the executioner was quite simply to execute, effectively and cleanly to carry out the sentence of the King. A failure to do so, to botch the job of punishment, would risk inciting the crowd to spare the life of the condemned man. And such a pardon was by sovereign right the exclusive province of the King. It was an instrument, symbolically perhaps the most important of the sovereign's right, crucial to the exercise of justice. The role of the executioner can be seen to presage that of the latter-day prisoner, who becomes a self-responsible agent in the dramaturgy of self-confession and knowledge.

The executioner communicated the truth of the crime to the assembled crowd through the body of the condemned man. If one were to ask why there was so much torture involved in executions one would find an answer in this communicative function. Foucault suggests that the renunciation of torture in the nineteenth century was closely connected to a shift in what was to be communicated through punishment. He argues that the latter-day practices sought "to put as much distance between the 'serene' search for truth and the violence that cannot be entirely effaced from punishment."[45] The two modes of truth that operated in the old regime and in the nineteenth century were incommensurate on logical as well as historical grounds—the former regime attached the truth of crime to the unbearable pressures of torture and the spectacle of public punishment; the latter to a consequential logic of causation independent of the infliction of pain.

The public execution itself was to be the source of this shift in the practices of truth. The mandatory assembling of people to be spectators to an execution, intended as a terroristic pedagogy, was an ambiguous phenomenon because as spectators they acted as participants in the proceedings.

> Not only must people know, they must see with their own eyes. Because they must be made afraid; but also because they must be the witnesses, the guarantors, of the punishment, and they must to a certain extent take part in it.[46]

Such a role was to give the people the opportunity to revolt, which is indeed what they sometimes did, especially when they found the verdict rendered against the criminal to be unjust. When the people assembled they were to hear the cries of the condemned, which were not always pleas for mercy but sometimes defiant curses against the judges and the laws. Sovereignty itself might be called into question.

During the eighteenth century, Foucault notes, there were many such disturbances centering around punitive practices. Authorities often cited these disturbances in their calls for reform. Public execution, in a way similar to the carnival's inversion of roles, "created centers of illegality."[47] The executions showed themselves increasingly to be a threat to authority on the part of the assembled people, who were expressing greater solidarity with those who were condemned. This solidarity, which decreased fear and increased defiance of sovereign authority, was in part a target of the penal reformers who called for an end to public executions.

With the decline of these executions, public attitudes toward crime and criminals were transformed. The once great and horrible crimes that somehow "belonged" to the people at large were transferred to a particular class of people. The broadsheets that advertised the heroic proportions of the acts of criminals (a genre that appeared and disappeared rapidly) gave rise, in its wake, to the first modern crime literature.

> The literature of crime transposes to another social class the spectacle that had surrounded the criminal. Meanwhile the newspapers took over the task of recounting the grey, unheroic details of everyday crime and punishment. The split was complete; the people was robbed of its old pride in its crimes; the great murders had become the quiet game of the well behaved.[48]

This transposition of famous crime had everything to do with the rise of the bourgeoisie, but it was not to be reduced to an "effect" of its dominance. Rather, it became a constitutive element in the differences that would find their expression under the newer arrangements of power. The earliest signs of what was to become normalization made their appearance in this categorization of criminality.

Punishment was to follow a course toward decreasing severity, it seemed, out of respect for the "humanity" of the criminal. But Foucault hastens to note that "the 'man' the reformers set up against the despotism of the scaffold has also become a 'man-measure': not of things, but of power."[49] Long before punishment became less severe, crimes themselves had changed in character and quality, becoming less violent. The growth in wealth in Europe during the early stages of market capitalism gave rise to new crimes, especially of vagabondage and theft against property. Many minor offenses came to the attention of magistrates, the laws concerning theft were made stricter, and the implementation of law was made more regular. All of this was done in response to the dissemination of the belief in a dramatic rise in crime and a belief that there need be "a law that was more restrained in its use of violence" so that it would be more readily available to be used.[50]

But for Foucault, much more than a simple rise in prosperity incited the shift away from attention on great crimes and toward the proliferation of lesser ones. Reformers were to be successful in their endeavor because of a strange coincidence: the severity of punishment was closely tied to the irregularity of its implementation. Such inconsistency was the underlying reason for the great mandate given to such reformers as Howard and Beccaria, when they suggested that certainty of punishment, not severity, was the way to ensure that the laws would be obeyed. The source of this irregularity has been little noted, even though it rests at the heart of Foucault's analysis of the breakup of the old way of punishing. The problem of the organization of judicial power lay in the multiplicity of jurisdictions that had sprung up as a result of several interlocking developments: the private appropriation of power, the confusion of the dispensing of justice and the making of law and, finally, the existence of too many privileges outside of common law.[51] The irony is that the conditions that produced a multiplicity of jurisdictions served to cancel each other out. Foucault comments that, as a result, "the criticism of the reformers was directed not so much at the weakness or cruelty of those in authority, as at a bad economy of power."[52]

This "bad economy" of power could be traced back to a central excess that was to be found in the identification of the right of punishment with the personal power of the sovereign. The difficulty was that the power of kings was eroding. Starting as early as the sixteenth century and intensifying during the course of the eighteenth century, kings would sell off their sovereign rights by auctioning offices. They did so to raise the increasing amounts of money necessary for their imperial projects and for the maintenance of the royal lifestyle. The auctioning of offices created magistrates who owned their own offices, and kings, using their power to do so, were constantly creating new offices to finance their adventures. This development further confused lines of authority back to the Crown. Moreover, in attempting to control what they had released, kings closely monitored those they appointed, creating counterappointments to redress previous imbalances and to check those to whom they had sold off some of their sovereignty. These interventions led to a justice that was arbitrary, overblown in the exercise of sovereign right at a time when the need for a less complicated standard was perceived to be of necessity.

It was not so much, or not only, the privileges of justice, its arbitrariness, its archaic arrogance, its uncontrolled rights that were criticized; but rather the mixture of its weaknesses and excesses, its exaggerations and loopholes, and above all the very principle of this mixture, the "super-power" of the monarch.[53]

It is clear for Foucault that the reformers were responding not to a general increased sensitivity to the horrors of punishment but to a political situation that called forth new strategies in the face of the increasing irregularity of punishment. The idea was "not to punish less, but to punish better; to punish with an attenuated severity perhaps, but in order to punish with more universality and necessity; to insert the power to punish more deeply into the social body."[54]

In short, what was happening during this period of the eighteenth century was a crisis as much in the field of illegality as in the legal order that presided over the illegal. Under the old order, differing levels of illegality were tolerated in each social strata. Those lowest in society possessed no *rights*, but there was, Foucault suggests, "a space of toleration" for the commission of illegalities.[55] And these illegalities were necessary for life to be tolerable for the lowest classes of people. Illegalities at other levels were also tolerated. There was a general sense throughout society concerning the degrees and levels of toleration that would be acceptable, and the infliction of punishment was evaluated in the assembled crowds in reference to these general and public judgments concerning the appropriateness of punishment. There was, in fact, a range of popular illegalities up to the mid-eighteenth century. The space of illegalities was a space in which freedom was exercised.

Foucault asserts that a crisis in popular illegality occurred during the middle of the eighteenth century. This crisis stemmed directly from, or was a part of, the enclosure crises. The redefining of property entailed in the dramatic transfer of the right to exist or have common access to particular spaces moved dramatically toward the emergent privileged class (a class composed of many of those who were also purchasing the sovereign right to punish) and away from those who had enjoyed not rights but the discretionary enjoyment of "tolerated illegalities." Those whose crimes had been tolerated when they were committed against the rights and privileges of others were punished with increasingly severe penalties when the general rights of those in the more privileged strata to a privileged access to lands were transformed into this more restrictive, more "useful" notion of property. In short, the broad toleration of illegality came to an end. "The illegality of rights, which often meant the survival of the most deprived, tended, with the new status of property, to become an illegality of property."[56] Again, "The illegality of property was separated from the illegality of rights."[57]

At work here is the conjunction of the two spaces of discipline and sovereign right. The conflicts brought about by the shifting dynamics of their interactions were to create extraordinary disorder in the transition to the modern age. The most identifiable dynamic force in this movement was this older sovereign power itself, a force so absolute and yet so irregular and personal that it "left its subjects free to practice a constant illegality; this illegality was like the correlative of this kind of power."[58] Hence, any attack on sovereign power was also an attack on the functions of this zone of tolerated illegality. To reduce the one was to reduce the other. Penal reformers were able to challenge both simply by calling for a more humane treatment of those accused of crime. At the intersection of two unlike spaces, they were soon to construct the heterotopia of the penitentiary, a new institutional space in which practices of freedom might come to be realized.

In doing so, they were the primary movers in the migration of sovereignty from King to a more generalizable area of administration, a key moment in the history of what Foucault later was to call the exercise of governmentality. "Penal reform," he writes, "was born at the point of junction between the struggle against the super-power of the sovereign and the infra-power of acquired and tolerated illegalities."[59] The paradox for the King was that he needed to attack elements of tolerated illegality (smuggling, especially), and yet every new attack weakened his power, strengthening the opposition to this increasingly incoherent exercise of power.[60] The end of public execution was among the very first of the reforms to take hold precisely because it was the most powerful, and hence volatile, conjunction of the unlimited power of the sovereign and the active illegality of the people.

More generally, the reformers sought to replace completely the old system not only in the revolutions that were to overcome the old sovereign but in the charting of a new domain over which a new sovereignty would reign. They would establish a new economy of punishment and administer illegalities differentially. In their reform efforts they would do more than that; they would establish a new regime in which the control of illegality would transform what it meant to be a subject. They would moderate punishment, setting limits upon the exercise of sovereign power. They would achieve a new calculus of punishment, designed to be gentle in its application, calling forth a respect for humanity out of the sense that such is the best way to control people. As the sovereignty of the King encouraged the existence of one sort of subject, the new sovereignty would encourage another. The migration of sovereignty, then, is not to be understood as simply a movement from one place to another but as a repositioning of a series of power arrangements that in the dynamic of their new interaction resulted in the creation of a new arrangement of spaces in which to be human.

Disciplinary Space

The rise of discipline was made possible in part by the establishment of what Foucault calls the "semio-techniques" of the new punishment, techniques that emerged in the wake of the decline of spectacle. The purpose of these—primarily signaled by the regularization of sentencing and the abolition of juridical torture—was to represent the new punishments as much as they were to be new instructions in the infliction of pain. An adequate representation of punishment's purposes was needed because there was no clarity concerning a political teleology of gentler punishment without one. Whereas in the drawing and quartering of a criminal there was never a doubt of the meaning of punishment—it was to show the majesty of the sovereign power, to make the pain of punishment so horrible that the witnesses would appreciate anew the majesty of the Crown—the new punishment was meant to be "forward looking." Under the new punishment's regime, there would be no way to account for the enormity of some crimes. This shift was of little concern because the shifts in the vicissitudes of political economy made "great crimes" less the source of a threat to the legitimacy of governance. The irrelevance of great crimes, in fact, comes about in large measure as a result of the withdrawal of the *supplice* as a means of determining the enormity of the crime. In part because it helped diffuse the power of great crimes, the new punishment would seek to focus on effects, seek to prevent recurrence of smaller offenses rather than to exact vengeance for great challenges to authority. As Foucault puts it, in this new regime of punishment, "One must punish exactly enough to avoid repetition."[61]

Beginning his discussion of discipline by sharply focusing attention on the manner of its representation, Foucault underlines the importance of the communicative role that punishment must serve in the preservation of a political order. This struggle always concerns the construction of analogies that will establish the fictive grounds allowing one to act—making less arbitrary what always has at its core an element of the contingent. How is one to determine the adequacy of a punishment? The migration of sovereignty, among other things, shows how arbitrary the infliction of punishment might be. Punishment needed to be made to appear less arbitrary. The new model struggled to place its faith in the representational schemes that were congruent with the rationality of Enlightenment. A calculus came into play, designed to reorient punishment in a particular direction, to enable the realization of control over behavior rather than the elimination of a force hostile to the sovereign. For Foucault, this calculus was as much one of appearance as it was of substance. Indeed, for Foucault, it is impossible to render such a distinction, which is why it is crucial to understand the force of punishment in such terms.

This project of gentle punishment required the diminution of great criminals and the establishment of a field of criminality that would be latent in the social body as a whole. Foucault lists a series of "rules" that would have as their overall effect the simultaneous individualization of crime and the generic qualifying of criminality. Criminality was to become the new object of penal intervention. Criminals were to be the objects of intervention, of psychiatric designations, of separation from the remainder of society in penitentiaries. But crime too was to become objectified. Reformers were to call for strategies and tactics in the social organization of space and the dynamics of policy that would present, against the old anonymity of those on the margins, a model of freedom that would begin to define it as a form of responsibility, on the one hand, and as a possession, on the other. When one has a property in one's self, one becomes a body capable of alienation, imprisoned by the demands of the logic of possessive desire, by the demands of the embryonic modern soul. The elevation of property as a right was to serve, then, as the catalyst for the transformation of the meaning of crime, criminal, and the knowing and responsible citizen.

This transformation can be traced through the body, which is the continuous site of the effects of punishment, but the body was, during the course of the reforms, to become subject to "individualizing" punishment. As extraordinarily focused as the punishment of torture was, its focus was on the crime, not the criminal, on the juridical subject, not the obedient subject. The gentle punishments that were to serve as the temporal linkage to the new disciplinary society initially operated in the field of signs, operating to publicize the advantages of obedience and the disadvantages of criminality, in short, setting in motion the processes through which the juridical subject might be made obedient to the power of a pedagogy of signs. Punishment itself was to turn inward upon the minutia of everyday life in order to change the habits of the subject. The application of punishment was thus to bypass the extant fields of representation and instead begin to touch the body in its materiality—"Exercises, not signs: timetables, compulsory movements, regular activities, solitary meditation, work in common, silence, application, respect, good habits."[62] This focus was to make the idea of the spectacle disappear, since there could be no use for it. In its place, a new institution was to emerge, one that would carry its own symbolic power: the prison was to be born as a vehicle for housing the new, obeying, docile subject.

From his study of these pedagogies of punishment, Foucault suggests there were three ways of organizing the power to punish at the end of the eighteenth century, one old and two new. The old mode of the spectacle was confronted with two alternative modes of utility. One of the new modes of punishment understood punishment as a system for requalifying individuals as juridical subjects; the other understood punishment as a system for coercing individuals and sought to set up a separate administration for subjecting the body to training.

> We have then, the sovereign and his force, the social body and the administrative apparatus; mark, sign, trace; ceremony, representation, exercise; the vanquished enemy, the juridical subject in the process of requalification, the individual subjected to immediate coercion; the tortured body, the soul with its manipulated representations, the body subjected to training.[63]

One might ask what constituted the great eighteenth-century alternative to the form of discipline that was to emerge. Foucault lays out his categories with a deep consistency: this middle category of penal alternatives consists of the social body, sign, representation, the requalification of the juridical subject, and the soul with its manipulated representations. These were to compose the various forces at work in a constitutional pedagogy, establishing a democratic education designed to gently persuade a constituency of the desirability of a sovereign order in which they might be the participants. The radical bourgeoisie of France and the emergent United States, the Enlightenment philosophers and the practical critics, joined together to create the sort of motivational machinery through which participation would be presumed enough, through which a requalification of the subject would be *sought* by the subject in danger. Yet the era was creating another sort of subject, one not interested in the quest for requalification, one not invested in the pedagogy afforded by Rousseau (and Paine) and Diderot (and Rush).[64]

Why did the prison, with its exercise of bodies, become the dominant form of punishment in the modern age? Is it only the inadequacy of this social pedagogy that is to blame? Or was the turn toward the minutia of training the subtle force that undermined the radical bourgeois utopia of reasonable order?

There is no certain and certainly no complete answer to this question. Paradoxically, the emergence of discipline is contingent on a number of factors, a series of specific responses to particular needs. While the emergence of disciplinary society could be comprehended as the culmination of a variety of improvised solutions that became available to the same field of knowledge due to their common meeting ground in the bodies of those who were not previously visible or necessary for modern governments to function, Foucault attributes its rise to the solutions proposed to problems associated with several autonomous realms of social life. These problems were, first, the development of large armies, which were composed in part from the ranks of dispossessed vagabonds who were thrown off the common lands during the enclosures; second, the growth in frequency of contagious diseases associated with the rapid growth of urban areas; and third, the increased need for literacy associated with the increased availability of books and the requirements of business. In turn, these needs resulted in the emergence of dressage and other drills, techniques of segmenting and isolating individuals, and changes in pedagogic techniques in schools. In North America, the sources for such changes were, if anything, more intensely a result of the need for attention to the movements of bodies.[65] There were many variations on these developments, but the general direction of innovations focused on a need to control bodily functions.

The body, because of its sensitive role as a sign, its increasing importance in the economy of capitalism, its vulnerability to the diseases that accompany radical population growth, its role in the realization of political strategies of nation-states, and most of all (and in need of mention because of its deceptive obviousness), *precisely because it is the body,* that is, because it is the both the object of these strategies and the means through which they are realized, was to be the site where the working out of the problems associated with these developments occurred.[66] The multiplicity of problems associated with the body and the solutions that were to be proposed were to establish both a political anatomy of the body and a mechanics of its movement. "The human body was entering a machinery of power that explores it, breaks it down and rearranges it."[67] The art of discipline was to be composed of mechanisms for attending to the little details establishing control over the postures of bodies, their movements, and their placement. Bodies were to be distributed in spaces. Spaces were to be controlled through the establishment of clear entries and exits, through the partitioning of rooms, through the establishment of specific functions for different spaces, through the ranking of the importance of spaces.[68] Activities were to be controlled through the use of timetables, establishment of schedules for the completion of tasks, exercises to correlate bodies and gestures, development of machines that would interact with bodies, and finally through processes that would account for every act and attempt to fill each moment to provide for an exhaustive use of time.[69] Schooling was to be organized into sequences that had a logic of progression to them, that reached to an indefinite set of goals, that would be incomplete in the realization but always within a clearly defined horizon.

Such a system of alternative education, one that depends not upon a rhetoric of persuasive speech but upon the monotony of repetitive exercises, presumes a genesis of human imaginative capacity, a point of origin from which any progress could be marked. Subjects become educated into a new mode of thinking about time, one not enclosed by the cycles of the seasons but opened toward the marking of segments of duration and aiming toward a notion of progress. "Power," Foucault writes, "is directly articulated onto time."[70] When he writes this he is referring us to the varieties of the imaginary capacity we have developed to remember and the distinct manner in which we have learned to impose order upon that memory. Disciplinary methods thus reveal a linear time whose movements are integrated, focused, and oriented to terminal and stable points. In short, the duality of anatomy and mechanics, or perhaps the intersection between the two, establishes a dynamic through which the body would be made useful, through which it would be dramatically energized.

In his discussion of the processes through which the body is made docile, Foucault provides a window for understanding the practical conditions that allow for the development of what might be called a free imagination. Through the migration of the King's sovereignty, imagination is loosened from the fetters of the duality of medieval political theology. Although the introduction of a new elementary understanding of power—power is to be located at the level of the infrastructure of subjectivity and is to come to inhabit bodies, to rise from within them—is often understood in terms of repression, Foucault is at pains to focus not only on how such a power shapes and defines who we are, but how it operates historically, informing the dynamics of the processes through which individuals are made into objects, operating to make subjects more dynamic, more useful, even as their lives are to be reorganized around norms. For instance, with the rise of militarized mobilizations of bodies, the notion of mass as a sign of power gave way to the idea of the effective distribution of force. Efficiency in operations began to come about through practices of vertical cooperation (Foucault notes this development in relationship to Marx's insight concerning vertical cooperation in *Capital*[71]), the synchronization of movement, and the mobilization of productive labor in the service of a larger goal. At this time, the body began the process of submitting to the power of organization. The body is coerced as it is individualized so as to be put to better use in collective projects. This coercion is ancillary to the thought that focuses on the social body. Foucault writes, "While jurists or philosophers were seeking in the pact a primal model for the construction or reconstruction of the social body, the soldiers and with them the technicians of discipline were elaborating procedures for the individual and collective coercion of bodies."[72]

The development of a normalizing judgment was to affect profoundly the emergence of disciplinary society even as normalization itself was to be one of disciplinary society's most profound innovations. The corporeality that informed the spectacle is reduced through normalizing practices to a "physicality" that is subtly more powerful than the spectacle it replaces because it relies upon the continuous application of pressure. "At the heart of all disciplinary systems," Foucault suggests, "functions a small penal mechanism."[73] This mechanism constitutes the remaining connection to the body, ensuring a place for it even as the touch of punishment becomes lighter and lighter. Normalization is actually made possible by this light touch; every deviation from the norm becomes subject to punishment because punishment itself becomes much less severe. Normalization operates as the principle that enunciates the extent of deviation and, in enunciating, provides both a directive for reducing the deviation and sustaining it. Indeed, through normalization a continuous power is exerted on the body. "The perpetual penality that traverses all points and supervises every instant in the disciplinary institutions compares, differentiates, hierarchizes, homogenizes, excludes. In short, it *normalizes*." This force was what Foucault was to call, in distinction to legal codes, "the penality of the norm."[74]

But if the normalized body is a coerced body, it is also a body that is placed into a temporal frame that demands that one imagine oneself as a free subject of a particular kind. The emergence of discipline, if not its culmination, depends upon the knowledge of a freedom associated with what might be called a zone of subjectivity, in which the individual subject is reoriented away from the relatively protected and secure cycles of feudal life and made to participate in the open-ended and fearful life composed of useful projects.[75] One might say that disciplinary society is in large measure born of the fear of disorientation that results from the knowledge of this open space. Of course, it is also deeply associated with the ordering principles that need to govern a society in which capitalism is the driving economic force. But to think that capitalism, as theorized in totalistic terms, is the cause of such a movement is, for Foucault, to move too quickly to reducing an ensemble of forces to a single cause. Such a theoretical move, by concentrating on one element of the operations of power, is to "mistake" the part for the whole.

Such a misrecognition is no mere scholarly error. Instead, for Foucault, the mistake is productive of meaning. Indeed, it might be said that disciplinary society emerges as a product of this mistake, this misrecognition of space. One must not say that discipline is a consequence of Marxism, or classical economics, but that it is a companion expression of the Enlightenment desire to organize and place into visibility the range of human experience. To put it another way, discipline can be understood as a primary consequence of a metonymic displacement of partial and open space with the enclosed and theoretically complete space of its exemplary institutions of control.[76] Discipline is the inevitable accompaniment of liberal strategies for establishing a ground. Such strategies inevitably engage in these moves of displacement, substituting the part for the whole, yet always, of course, incompletely. The founders of disciplinary society engaged in a replication of the epistemological move that must be followed to comprehend even the most famously obvious instance of metonymy, that of the Crown's displacement of the King. (It is no small irony that this common dictionary example of metonymy applies so aptly to the problem of the sovereignty's migration. The dictionary, after all, emerged in the late eighteenth and early nineteenth centuries as a device of normalization through the standardization of pronunciation and spelling.[77]) The mistake itself becomes a part of the truth of the modern way of practicing freedom.

But the practice of establishing that truth has its own rigor. The "means of correct training," as Foucault labels it, established a set of techniques for marking the body as a text and then for allowing a generalization from textuality to corporeality to be made. The techniques that give rise to a direct articulation of power upon time—segmentation, serialization, synthesis, and totalization[78]—techniques that made it possible to imagine new practices of continuous control, would be realized practically with the emergence of these "textual" techniques for inscribing power upon bodies through training. Although this process was undoubtedly "fictional," in the sense of imposing its force upon society through the pretend devices of contractual association and autonomous individuality, it was also, for all its fictionality, real, as the product and fulfillment of its promise. "The individual," Foucault writes, in one of the most famous passages from this book,

> is no doubt the fictitious atom of an "ideological" representation of society;
> be he is also a reality fabricated by this specific technology of power that I
> have called "discipline." We must cease once and for all to describe the
> effects of power in negative terms: it "excludes," it "masks," it "represses,"
> it "censors," it "abstracts," it "masks," it "conceals." In fact, power produces;
> it produces reality; it produces domains of objects and rituals of truth. The
> individual and the knowledge that may be gained of him belong to this
> production.[79]

The power that produces the individual is disciplinary, but that does not mean that it is singular, unitary, or closed. Domains of objects and rituals of truth emerge from a series of practices that compensate for the collapse of previously settled practices, practices that had served similar purposes in their time. Each practical exercise rests upon the body, training it, securing it, focusing its energies in new ways. Modernity as a practical matter, as the ordinary exercise of freedom, was under way.

The paradoxical process of training was to culminate in what Foucault called, in his discussion of panopticism, "an epistemological 'thaw' through a refinement of power relations."[80] Discipline crossed a threshold, that is, became essential to practice, as the result of a multiplication of the power effects of training and their articulation as a new reality principle. Discipline became intrinsic to practice as a result of an accumulation of knowledge upon the bodies subjected to the new microphysics of power. In crossing over the threshold, we might say into modernity, disciplinary society was to articulate the new reality.

These techniques have been minutely attended to in the critical literature concerning Foucault. His detailed descriptions of hierarchical observation, normalizing judgment, the examination, especially as they culminate in the imaginary architecture figure of the Panopticon, which operates to redistribute the power gathered together through the network of these practices, prompted the criticisms of totalization that I mentioned in the introduction to this chapter. But such criticisms are largely rooted in a profound misunderstanding of the meaning of the Panopticon for both Bentham and Foucault. This misunderstanding has to do with the meaning of the Panopticon as an exemplar of power/knowledge.

It could be that the most important element of Foucault's analysis of power in *Discipline and Punish* remains unstated in the book itself. For unless we are to believe that Foucault understands the operations of power to be the perfect realization of an absolute system of control—a belief that must ignore the constant references to resistance that are found throughout his work—we can best realize the meaning of Foucault's presentation of Bentham's Panopticon as that of being a heterotopia. Because it is important for the thinking of the prison as a space, we might remember that among the principles of heterotopias is that of a spatial control over time to make the particular experience of time take on special qualities. But it is also crucial to recall that heterotopias are not only intensifications of spaces of time. They are also both separated from and connected to the remainder of the experience of space through a variety of barriers and passages. Heterotopias operate to displace space, which means that they never operate without having an impact on the space that remains.

> Either their role is to create a space of illusion that exposes every real space, all the sites inside of which human life is partitioned, as still more illusory. . . . Or else, on the contrary, their role is to create a space that is other, another real space, as perfect, as meticulous, as well arranged as ours is messy, ill-constructed, and jumbled.[81]

The fear that animates the establishment of the heterotopia of the Panopticon is precisely that of subjects living in open-ended space. Foucault expressed this fear as an anxiety. He believes "that the anxiety of our era has to do fundamentally with space, no doubt a great deal more than with time."[82]

If one compares Foucault's comments on the qualities of heterotopias of compensation with the figure of Bentham's Panopticon, one might better see how the analysis of the organizing forces of modernity is deeply influenced by his understanding of the social constitution of space itself.[83] Segmentation, serialization, synthesis, and totalization are all spatial articulations of power. The Panopticon is a building that ideally achieves the goal of perfect surveillance over those who are enclosed within its walls by bringing together in a single space all of these modes of correction. It is circular and multistoried, with cells that face to a central tower which has an unimpeded view of each room. Each person in it is isolated from all other persons, yet all are potentially visible from the central tower. The purpose of this surveillance is to disallow deviant behavior on the part of abnormal individuals. Confined in a cell, exposed to the gaze of a supervisor, the individual is "the object of information, never a subject in communication."[84] The individual is seen but never sees those who watch.

The purpose of the Panopticon is not only to secure a separation of the abnormal from the normal. It is to dissipate abnormality as it distributes normalcy: in distributing the normal, it creates new norms. "Thanks to its mechanisms of observation, it gains in efficiency and in the ability to penetrate into men's behavior; knowledge follows the advances of power, discovering new objects of knowledge over all the surfaces on which power is exercised."[85] The polyvalence of its application—factories, schools, and hospitals as well as prisons were to be organized under panopticism's principles—establishes it as the spatial expression of the positive project of power. "The panoptic mechanism is not simply a hinge, a point of exchange between a mechanism of power and a function; it is a way of making power relations function, and a way of making a function through these power relations."[86] Panopticism is a generalized function of disciplinary society, an "intensificator of power."[87]

As a heterotopia, the Panopticon's peculiar quality is that of being the spatial mode of power that is most fully responsive to the general anxiety about space itself. The Panopticon is itself indefinitely generalizable, never completely realized; as a heterotopia, it must be posed against the messiness of the spaces its displaces. The Panopticon operates at the level, and precisely in the opposite direction, of the figure of power that it displaces, that of the King. If the King's body transmitted power vertically, panopticism disperses it horizontally. If the body of the King was limited in its presence, able to deploy its power only through the vitiation of its singular strength, panopticism makes a strength out of stillness, concerning itself with the lower domain of irregularity and individuality on the scale of multiplicities of bodies. Panopticism, then, becomes the general operating principle of what will become disciplinary society. It is a heterotopia of heterotopias, and if we accept Foucault's claim that "there is probably not a single culture in the world that fails to constitute heterotopias," its dissemination is coterminus with at least one modality of the globalizing tendencies in modern political culture.[88]

Foucault notes the power of panopticism as a mode of organizing reality in an aphorism: "A real subjection is born mechanically from a fictitious relation."[89] The fictitious relation is one of an imaginary surveillance, an externally induced internal state of mind. Foucault shows how the heterotopic link provided by Panopticism connects the external world to the internal world by building upon the core presupposition of all heterotopias, that of being "a system of opening and closing that both isolates [the heterotopia] and makes it penetrable."[90] The Panopticon is designed to go so far as to modify the connection between the inside and outside through its manipulation of the entries and exits that separate its space from the displaced remainder of the world. In effect, it is designed to make the world at large heterotopic, to generalize the principle of discrete space, to particularize the struggles concerning the shape and meaning of modern subjectivity, to allow the logic of compensation to inform the meaning of life at large.

Of course, general principles are not total institutions. There is a gap between the idea of the Panopticon as an exemplary institution and the function of that idea in the political imagination of disciplinary society. But the difficulty with comprehending the meaning of panopticism lies not only in its mistaken identity as a utopian principle but in the errors that arise from the failure to recognize that it exists as an "infraprinciple" of power, not a blueprint. Panopticism is the linchpin around which several crucial historical processes are able to communicate with each other, not an abstract principle against which human behavior is to conform. It provides an organizing rationale through which, as Foucault says, "the ordering of human multiplicities" might happen. It establishes a means through which a complex division of labor could be coordinated. The deployment of its principles throughout a polity is to occur rapidly—and yet peculiarly silently—as it appears as a minimal response to a pressing problem of disorder. As Bentham puts it, " 'Economy seated, as it were, upon a rock —the gordian knot of the Poor-Laws not cut, but untied—all by a simple idea in architecture!' "[91] Panopticism creates coherent connections between a negative freedom that establishes a space within which one is able to enjoy autonomy and the modes of control and coercion that are the synonym for positive liberty, upon which any sovereign order will continue to need to rely, long after the king is displaced as the representative of sovereign authority.[92] In this sense, disciplinary society is born of the need to secure the blessings of liberty. But the connections between security and liberty could not become overt. Panopticism thus provides a way in which the necessary objectification of subjects could be tolerated in a regime that was to hold the idea of individual right in great esteem.

The Panopticon provides order to multiplicities, connecting a heterogeneous variety of activities that were previously viewed as separate and encouraging the homogenization of separate spaces, not to bring them together but to make them more manageable. Consideration of all of these functions of the Panopticon leads Foucault to make perhaps his most radical claim in the final sentence of the chapter on panopticism. But even in assessing that claim he is careful not to reduce his meaning to a totalistic and draconian statement. He writes,

Is it surprising that the cellular prison, with its regular chronologies, forced labor, its authorities of surveillance and registration, its experts in normality, who continue and multiply the functions of the judge, should have become the modern instrument of penality? Is it surprising that prisons resemble factories, schools, barracks, hospitals, which all resemble prisons?[93]

If one presumes that panopticism expresses a simple utopian wish for perfect order, then there is much to dread in this formulation. In a utopian world, the principle of resemblance is purely and clearly communicated. A utopian world also allows for the development of its opposite, the dystopia. Dystopias share one crucial feature with utopias; the complete determination of conditions and outcomes of existence, the imagination of a place where power does not exist, only force. However, the function of a heterotopia in reference to representation is quite different. In a heterotopic space the circle of resemblance is never perfect. It operates not as an expression of linguistic clarity and perfection but, instead, as a series of displacements of the desire for perfection. The desire for order is always only partially completed, always deferred to the next location, and is communicated along the imperfect lines of resemblance. The irony of disciplinary society is that the modern prison functions as the most complete realization of this principle of incompleteness.

This principle of incompleteness (if one elevates it to a principle), as will be seen, often informs the function of delinquency in a rebarbative and frightening manner, suggesting that the techniques of disciplinary society are both more insidious and more deep-seated than they might initially seem to be. But this principle of incompleteness is also the linchpin within the key Foucaultian notion of resistance, to which any idea of freedom must be attached. As there is no power without resistance, there is no resistance without freedom. It is the style of such freedom that must be questioned, not its existence. And such questioning continues to concern the sort of politics that adheres to a freedom that operates as a form of resistance.

Delinquency, Normalization, Indiscipline

"The theme of the Panopticon," Foucault writes, "—at once surveillance and observation, security and knowledge, individualization and totalization, isolation and transparency—found in the prison its privileged locus of realization."[94] That the prison is to be such a site may not be surprising, in retrospect. But one might also reflect upon what it means to suggest that the machinery of panopticism finds its best initial location in the prison, if only because the control over experience suggested by panopticism was to radiate outward from the interior exclusion of the prison.

The logic seems obvious. The prison is the site of a confinement to the outside. This confinement itself is the modern penitentiary experience. Within the walls of prisons convicts find themselves paradoxically suffering the punishment of banishment, a removal, an internal exile from the quotidian that constitutes the life that is displaced by their removal from it. The mundane substance of the prison schedule—work, silence, isolation, repetition—gives the texture of such a life its own quotidian quality, forms the rituals that provide the constitutive framework for the surplus of discipline, which consequently can be measured against the baseline of the prison experience as simple detention.[95] And it is true that the discipline that exceeded the minimum constraints required for detention is precisely that which develops an ensemble of relations that are to be applied beyond prisons. Yet in the move from prisons to the outside, more than just the transfer of disciplinary technology is involved. Instead, what Foucault characterizes as an epistemological break occurs, a break having the effect of disturbing the older set of relations that prevail among the inhabitants of any particular social order.

The break concerns presumptions about what might be known of a subject and what might be done about the subject who is known. Foucault puts this matter directly when he writes that "the offender becomes an individual to know. . . . It is as a convict, as a point of application for punitive mechanisms, that the offender is constituted himself as the object of possible knowledge."[96] This object of possible knowledge is what comes to be called the *delinquent,* the person who is constituted as a criminal not only because of having committed a crime but because of being what he is. Foucault writes, "The correlative of penal justice may well be the offender, but the correlative of the penitentiary apparatus is someone other; this is the delinquent, a biographical unity, a kernel of danger, representing a type of anomaly."[97] The delinquent is not directly reachable by law but is reachable by the ancillary techniques of discipline. The life of the criminal, his biography, becomes crucial to determining how he is to be treated by the forces of discipline. This *bio-graphic* imposition of power, this writing of a life on a body, gives tragicomic depth to the internal characteristics of otherwise anonymous beings. In narrativizing their motivational lives it marks them as martyrs to disciplinary power, associates them with the bourgeois radicals in a peculiar mirroring process, as the little criminals admired in the romances of more orderly advocates of freedom, as those who advance this radical bourgeois freedom through their outlaw ways.

The delinquent is to be captured at the intersection of penal and psychiatric discourses. Through this crossing of two knowledges, two heterotopic spaces intersect and create the possibilities of existence for this being, who becomes known as a dangerous individual. Rather than someone who has merely broken the law and must be punished, he is understood as a criminal character because of his fit into a psycholegal category. He *is* a criminal because of his fit into a typology of characteristics, which makes him capable of particular actions. All that we need wait for is the commission of the criminal act itself, and as the apparatuses of disciplinary society expand, we need no longer wait: we have devices that can intervene below the level of sovereignty, that are compatible with sovereign right, and that enable delinquents to be touched by a normalizing power. The moment of reassurance engendered in this discourse of criminology is to be found in the rhetorical move that enables us to imagine a life script for the criminal deviant, the most unpredictable of modern beings, that paradoxically will be followed in predictable, or at least calculable, ways. The delinquent is the dangerous, but the dangerous under the sign of the anomaly, that is to say, the criminal is made familiar, subjected to a knowledge that will make his actions explicable and reasonable.

Yet the establishment of the characteristics upon which these predictions will be made and will be borne out does not conflict with or efface the idea of individual responsibility for actions, as it does, for instance, when applied to the discourse of insanity. It is far too dangerous to evoke the notion of madness alone in characterizing the criminal. Madness still evokes a radical otherness, a possibility that the reason and predictability of human order can be overturned. There is a risk involved in the evocation of madness, a risk of the unleashing of an unreason that psychiatry is specifically designed to silence. Even so, the criminal "type" is someone in between reason and its other, a known object, an exemplary figure of modernity.

In this way the body of the tortured criminal disappears and is replaced with the body of a prisoner with the "soul" of a delinquent—a soul fabricated by the very disciplinary forces that constrain him. What Foucault called "the non-corporeal reality of delinquency"[98] holds together the modern system of punishment as it holds the subjected body of the offender in place. Criminological discourse comes to concern itself with identifying and categorizing delinquencies and delinquents and developing the means through which they might be changed or controlled. It is at this point in the emergence of disciplinary society that the norm comes to displace the law as an organizing category for action. "Now the 'delinquent' makes it possible to join the two lines [of monstrosity and the juridical subject] and to constitute under the authority of medicine, psychology, or criminology, an individual in whom the offender of the law and the object of scientific technique are superimposed—or almost—one upon the other."[99]

Foucault emphasizes that criminological discourse does not operate as a response to delinquency but as a response to the delinquency that it establishes through its discourse. The prison fabricates delinquency through its objective powers of surveillance, through its techniques for individualizing, and through its capacity to correct. The prison mobilizes delinquency, making it useful for the larger disciplinary project by linking it to the dangerous otherness of madness. Thus there is a double aspect to delinquency. It is another product of the displacement of power but also one that functions to reenforce the normalizing discourse as its appropriate form of resistance. The disciplinary order is able to make the fact of delinquency crucial to modern being, to make the figure of the modern individual a disciplined subject—and an object of knowledge—not by the force of a violent and obvious repression but by the subtle power that operates through the association of delinquency with deviance from a norm. In this way the delinquent becomes an important object of a normalizing power, the margin that defines the center.

Understood in this way, the delinquent is perhaps the most abject figure to be found in modern societies, yet the delinquent also comes close to being the emblematic figure of freedom in that world. The delinquent bears the peculiar burden of standing for freedom within the confinements of the prison. The double figuring of the delinquent as both prisoner and transgressor puts the most elemental aspect of freedom on the margins of a social order that claims freedom as its most important value. Indeed, it contributes to an impoverished political imagination concerning freedom, in which the elements of freedom that are most untamed by the institutional and experiential forms that contain and support them and that rely most completely on the free play of power in conjunction with imagination are carefully segregated from the orderly and secure experiences of the least free dimensions of life.[100]

Yet this containment and marginalization of what might be called the neutral space of negative freedom by the proliferation of normalizing strategies actually operates as an incitement to free beings. On the face of it, of course, the prison has been a resounding failure. In every one of its incarnations it has failed to diminish crime, it has seemed to cause a marked "recidivism" among those who have inhabited it, it has produced delinquents, it has marked those who had been incarcerated so as to discourage their reintegration into "society," and it indirectly has encouraged more crime by throwing entire families into destitution and reconfiguring the base relationships among family members. But from the birth of the prison the logic of delinquency requires its reproduction in terms compatible with the critique of the effects that it produces. Whereas at the level of the individual, delinquency operates as a *lack,* as a condition to be avoided, at the level of the institution of technologies of punishment, delinquency incites a criticism that encourages two seemingly opposite but consequentially identical responses that reproduce and intensify the hold of delinquency (and of discipline) over society. First, the failure of prisons to reduce delinquency implied that they were not sufficiently corrective. Alternatively, the failure of the prisons indicated that they were not sufficiently punitive. Foucault notes,

> The answer to these criticisms was invariably the same: the reintroduction of the invariable principles of penitentiary technique. For a century and a half the prison had always been offered as its own remedy: the reactivation of the penitentiary techniques as the only means of overcoming their perpetual failure; the realization of the corrective project as the only method of overcoming the impossibility of implementing it.[101]

In short, the failure of the prison is part of its function within the larger carceral system. That system, composed not only of the prison and the techniques of training internal to it but of a whole series of auxiliary institutions and techniques that provide a network for connecting the prison to the remainder of society, provides the modern world with its distribution of offenses and penalties. It establishes the modern economy of illegalities. That economy, once open and indefinite, appears to be closed not because of its containment within a horizon of "necessity" but because the circulation of its elements is determined strategically within the horizon of disciplinary society.

But the appearance is deceptive. Delinquency becomes a linchpin connecting the dramatic proliferation of normalizing categories to the older kinds of illegality. The indefinite character of the place of any individual within the categories of the "norm" ensures that there will always be deviations from it. While one might focus on how normalization operates to constrain, to establish a fundamental insecurity concerning being, one might also note that the very same strategy can show individuals how happenstance their individuality is, how it is constituted through the establishment of small measures, each of which in itself is not decisive in the formation of a person's life but all of which determine its shape. In the negotiations of being that are enabled through the various tactical resistances to normalization available to us, we might learn to refuse ourselves, to resist who we are. Such is the role given the delinquent.

Discipline itself activates delinquency even as it generates political responses to it. In the circumstances that inform its establishment and perpetuation, delinquency becomes that which both surrounds and contains illegality because the final consequence of the development of delinquency is the extension of the techniques of surveillance to the population at large. Those illegalities still tolerated are accepted not as social relations that are beneath the view or notice of sovereign authority but as minor infractions that in and of themselves notify authorities of the larger delinquency that remains at large. Because there is a deep concern with the prevention of crime and because crime is associated with types of people who may or may not be caught violating the law itself, license is given for the creation of a new societal force, the police. "Delinquency, with the secret agents that it procures, but also with the generalized policing that it authorizes, constitutes a means of perpetual surveillance of the population: an apparatus that makes it possible to supervise, through the delinquents themselves, the whole social field."[102] A circuit is completed, which the course of Western societies has not broken since, from the police to the prison to delinquency to the police to the prison to delinquency. . . .

This process is an incitement to the freedom that is contained within the production of delinquency. The powers that might be found within the transgressions of the law of sovereignty are those that are fueled by the very power of discipline. Sovereignty seeks to contain within a field of discipline the disorder that is both the threat to its power and its source. To protect its rights from the freedom that is the source of its power, the sovereign order participates in the dissemination of freedom in the form of delinquency. The network of surveillance established through discipline, the social circuitry of illegalities and delinquencies, lends itself to new resistances even as it renders older ones obsolete. What does not become obsolete is the freedom that is generated through resistance to order, the transgressive impulse that comes into play through the very establishment of limits.

Toward the conclusion of *Discipline and Punish* Foucault suggests how such resistances to discipline might arise from within the system itself. He presents a story concerning the sentencing of an offender.[103] In 1840, a thirteen-year-old went before a judge and in response to the judge's question "What is your station?" suggested that a station in life is a form of slavery. "Oh, a good house, an apprenticeship, it's too much trouble. And anyway, the bourgeois . . . always grumbling, no freedom."[104] For Foucault, this exchange between offender and judge marked a confrontation that was at the time emerging between the law—which had come to envelope illegality in the larger system of discipline-penality-delinquency—and an illegality that could only be called "indiscipline." "Confronted with discipline on the face of the law, there is illegality, which puts itself forward as a right; it is indiscipline, rather than criminal offence, that causes the rupture."[105] This indiscipline is the Doppelganger of disciplinary society. It is both opposed to discipline and impossible without it. It proliferates on the boundaries of every experience touched by the disciplines themselves and remains a trace by which one might gauge the transformed circumstances of social life. The vagabond demonstrates an indiscipline of language, an indiscipline of immediate liberty, and an indiscipline in family relations. The vagabond is an anonymous and undisciplined individual, an amalgam of discipline and the possibilities of resistance to discipline engendered by its domination. The presence of the vagabond (and the vagabond's successors) suggests that the resources for the resistance to disciplinary society are not to be unearthed in formal freedoms, that is, the rights permitted by disciplinary regimes. Those rights, attached to the sovereignty of law, require clarity and coherence in their administration. In opposition to such rights, the vagabond's radical rejection of the claims of delinquency provided an incoherent resource through which order might be challenged and thwarted. What appeared to the journalists who recorded the exchange between judge and vagabond as the savagery of the prisoner, "living from day to day and with no tomorrow," was precisely the transgressive counter created by disciplinary regimes.

*   *   *

In his discussion of *Discipline and Punish,* Gilles Deleuze cautions readers not to misapprehend Foucault as a "thinker of confinement." He suggests that "Foucault has always considered confinement a secondary element derived from a primary function that was very different in each case."[106] Deleuze issues this caution in part because he wants to insist that an understanding of the general principles of confinement requires a recognition and appreciation of the realm of exteriority that shapes that which is confined and communicates to it the excesses that energize it. Deleuze cites Maurice Blanchot's comment regarding Foucault: "Confinement refers to an outside, and what is confined is precisely what is outside."[107] Disciplinary society can be located in the thought that established a way of confining this "outside." Panopticism expresses the power of this confinement, a confinement paradoxically capable of communicating itself across the social geography of all of what we might call modern experience. As it comes into play, its mark is to be felt by many. Illegality comes to be displaced by delinquency. Categories of experience come to be reorganized. The range of what is right and wrong begins to shift. The extent of the social order's capacity to organize and infiltrate the remainder of social experience grows, even as its effects become less obvious. The possibilities of transgressing the limits of such a society come to be reshaped in response to this general mobilization of disciplinary order.

But what does such a mobilization tell us? How we might evaluate Foucault's politics depends on our assessment of the relationship between discipline and indiscipline, because the character of Foucault's appreciation of freedom lies in his ability to identify its complex association with the forms of power. The presence of indiscipline in the figure of the vagabond suggests that the creation of disciplinary society does not result in the triumph of a totalistic logic but, instead, in something not closely tied to logic at all, to a will to knowledge that is ultimately opposed to power, associated with a desire for order and coherence. But that desire arises precisely as the expression of a lack that will not be fulfilled through any ordering principle. This lack signals something absolute about disciplinary society, namely, its fundamentally incomplete character, the disorder that exists at the heart of order itself. The desire that is informed by this lack is a result of the officially recognized form of freedom allowed by disciplinary society. Such a freedom, rooted in individual existence, is sufficiently transgressive when it is actually exercised. But the danger of disciplinary society is that it poses a deep risk of a decisive misidentification of freedom, not with individual existence, but with securing the continuity of the very order that would oppose individuality's continued existence. This is the risk of a repudiation of the fear that is necessarily involved in being free. We need to accept fear to be free.[108]

In the concluding chapter of *Discipline and Punish,* Foucault makes note of a problem of disciplinary society, one that involves the emergence of what he called "the supervision of normality." By this phrase, he means to suggest that a range of disciplines associated with psychology and its institutional supports in schools, hospitals, corporations, and governmental agencies work to "penetrate" indiscipline, to "normaliz[e] the power of normalization."[109] The steep rise in the use of mechanisms of normalization in a mature disciplinary order begins to blur the distinctions between prison and other elements of disciplinary society. This blurring is itself a danger in the wake of a century and a half of the individuation brought about through disciplinary society.

Here I am slightly ahead of myself. The problem of the normalization of norms is perhaps better discussed under the rubric "bio-power." The emergence of this more complete normalizing discourse is itself not neatly or completely separate from its own genealogy within disciplinary society. However, in working to normalize even that which resists normalization, in normalizing the forms of resistance as they emerge from delinquency, those who engage in contemporary exercises of power may have been able to put at risk more than just a mode of freedom but the very possibility of free existence itself. Normalizing the norm—is there a more succinct definition of cybernetics than that? Normalizing the norm—is this not the great (unannounced) end of the various strategies aimed at human extinction? A question that emerges for us at the end of the twentieth century is whether the style of freedom that has accompanied disciplinary society and that has been nurtured by it—and for the sake of brevity let us call that freedom liberal freedom—has itself been the reason leading humankind to this moment of terminal risk. But even if it has, this does not mean that liberal freedom has not been a way of being free. Instead, what it may suggest is that the freedom that has been so long associated with a particular organization under the banner of sovereign right may need to be rethought so that we may better understand and give shape to a politics of freedom more commensurate with the conditions of late modernity. I believe that this is what Foucault may be thinking when he urges us to rethink the form that the idea of right might take as sovereignty and normalization vitiate the very possibility of repression in a disciplinary age.

The birth of the prison is also the birth of the means through which it may be resisted. We should not, however, completely identify freedom as resistance, as deeply as freedom informs resistance. It is important to understand that we are free within the experience of discipline as well as in resistance to it. The activity of freedom is in part the activity of transgressing the boundaries between discipline and indiscipline, an activity that serves to create conditions through which the limits of the spatial arrangements engendered through disciplinary society can be assessed. But freedom is not exhausted by the clarification of its situation. Indeed, freedom is neither positive nor negative but something other than. Freedom may be likened to seduction: it is that which allows us to go on in the face of the pain that allows us to remember. The activity of freedom is what will enable us to meditate on a question that arises only in the wake of the conditions enabled and developed into maturity through disciplinary society: What modes of life, what styles of existence, are possible in an era when the great project of disciplinary society is drawing to a close?

Notes

1. Michel Foucault, *Discipline and Punish: The Birth of the Prison,* trans. Alan Sheridan (New York: Pantheon, 1977). On issues concerning Foucault's biography and reputation, I rely primarily on David Macey, *The Lives of Michel Foucault* (New York: Pantheon, 1993). There are two other important biographies of Foucault: Didier Eribon, *Michel Foucault,* trans. Betsy Wing (Cambridge, MA: Harvard University Press, 1991), and James Miller, *The Passion of Michel Foucault* (New York: Simon & Schuster, 1993). Although each of these books has its merits, Eribon's suffers from a lack of familiarity with the relevant philosophical texts and the intellectual history of them, and Miller's suffers from an obsession with Foucault's homosexuality and because of this monomania tends to reduce Foucault's work to a product of his personality, an approach decidedly at odds with Foucault's own sensibility.

2. Foucault elaborates on his understanding of Nietzsche most explicitly in "Nietzsche, Genealogy, History," in *Language, Counter-Memory, Practice: Selected Essays and Interviews,* ed. Donald Bouchard, trans. Donald F. Bouchard and Sherry Simon (Ithaca, NY: Cornell University Press, 1977), 139-64.

3. See Foucault, "The Discourse on Power," in *Remarks on Marx: Conversations with Duccio Trombadori,* trans. R. James Goldstein and James Casciato (New York: Semiotext(e), 1991), 147-81. "I have never presumed that 'power' was something which could explain everything. . . . *For me, power is that which must be explained*" (148).

4. See Friedrich Nietzsche, *The Birth of Tragedy and the Case of Wagner,* trans. Walter Kauffman (New York: Vintage, 1967), 18.

5. Ibid.

6. See "On Power," in *Michel Foucault: Politics, Philosophy, Culture,* ed. Lawrence Kritzman (New York: Routledge, 1988), 101.

7. For an assessment of the possibilities of "a left Nietzscheanism," see William E. Connolly, *Political Theory and Modernity* (New York: Basil Blackwell, 1988), 184, 188. I emphasize the fact that Foucault seeks to democratize the Nietzschean insight precisely because there are political theorists who both believe that Nietzsche is correct in his diagnosis of the problem of nihilism and yet seek to keep this knowledge hidden from the world at large for fear that democracy is itself nihilistic. Such a doctrinal teaching is advanced secretly by many of the students of Leo Strauss. It is, I think, a dangerously authoritarian teaching. For an overview of Strauss's political thought that focuses on this problem, see Shadia Drury, *The Political Thought of Leo Strauss* (New York: St. Martin's, 1989).

8. An essay on *Discipline and Punish* that pursues this connection to the themes in *On the Genealogy of Morals* is François Ewald's "Anatomie et corps politique," *Critique,* no. 343 (December 1975). Also see Macey, *The Lives of Michel Foucault,* 335-6.

9. Friedrich Nietzsche, *On the Genealogy of Morals and Ecce Homo,* ed. Walter Kauffman, trans. Walter Kauffman and R. J. Hollingdale (New York: Vintage Books, 1969), 57.

10. See *The Book of Job,* intro. and trans. Stephen Mitchell (San Francisco: North Point Press, 1987), 88. For a powerful analysis of the Jobian condition, see William E. Connolly, *The Augustinian Imperative* (Newbury Park, CA: Sage, 1993), esp. chap. 1, "Voices from the Whirlwind."

11. One might note how controversial the idea of putting punishment first is by examining a parallel (perhaps identical) controversy between two writers who might broadly be construed

as "liberal" in their perspective. See Elaine Scarry, *The Body in Pain: The Making and Unmaking of the World* (New York: Oxford University Press, 1986), and the review of that book by Judith Shklar in *London Review of Books,* 18 October 1986. Also see Shklar's *Ordinary Vices* (Cambridge, MA: Harvard University Press, 1984), esp. chap. 1, "Putting Cruelty First." Shklar vigorously attacks Scarry for making pain the center of her phenomenological investigation. She also excoriates others for doing the same in her essay on cruelty, understanding such a concern as perverse at worst and misanthropic at best. James Miller relies on Shklar's simple rejection of cruelty in an essay in which he attempts to address the problem of cruelty in Nietzsche and Foucault. See "Carnivals of Atrocity," *Political Theory* 18 (August 1990): 470-91. There, Miller is previewing his book on Foucault, one that, as I mentioned earlier, focuses on Foucault's personal life in order to criticize his philosophy. One wonders if the same approach could be used to develop a critique of Miller. See Miller, *The Passion of Michel Foucault.* In wondering about Miller's personal life, I am not trying to make an idle retort. I am, I think, responding to the mistaken idea that there should be an area of life not examined by political thinkers, a privileged arena of privacy. Foucault would have suggested, I think, that the examination of the self must be pursued relentlessly by the self in question. The difficulty with Shklar's (and Miller's) critique of cruelty is that it is directed entirely outward, proceeding encased in its own privilege, failing to note that cruelty attends even the attempt to condemn it or ignore it, and finally, failing to subject themselves to the same judgments.

For a more thorough critique of Shklar's "liberalism of fear," see Thomas L. Dumm, *united states* (Ithaca, NY: Cornell University Press, 1994).

12. Nietzsche, *Genealogy of Morals,* 58.

13. Ibid., 61.

14. Ibid., 64.

15. Ibid., 64-65. "The compensation, then, consists of a warrant for and title to cruelty." Nietzsche's understanding of the *logic* of compensation, if not the substantial conclusion regarding the turn to cruelty, is quite likely derived from his understanding of the philosophy of Ralph Waldo Emerson. Two essays are relevant here: Emerson's "Compensation" and "Experience," in his collections *Essays: First Series* and *Essays: Second Series.* The complete texts of both books can be found in Ralph Waldo Emerson, *Essays and Lectures* (New York: Library of America, 1984).

16. Nietzsche, *Genealogy of Morals,* 84. I think the primary contribution of the psychoanalytic tradition will be seen in this way. There have been people who have contributed to a critique of the contract in this regard. The first work that I know of that systematically explored its implications for liberal polities is John Wikse, *About Possession: The Self as Private Property* (University Park: Pennsylvania State University Press, 1977).

17. This question was raised for me by Richard Flathman. He might consider this paragraph a partial compensation for his steady engagement with an earlier draft of this chapter (if not a satisfactory response to his criticisms).

18. For a more thorough discussion of Berlin's theory of freedom, see Chapter 2.

19. Nietzsche, *Genealogy of Morals,* 65.

20. Foucault, *Discipline and Punish,* 16.

21. Ibid., 13.

22. On Jean Baudrillard's view concerning embodiment and its limits, see esp. *Simulations,* trans. Paul Foss, Paul Patton, and Philip Beitchman (New York: Semiotext(e), 1983).

23. Foucault, *Discipline and Punish,* 16.

24. Ibid., 19.

25. Ibid., 22.

26. Ibid., 24.

27. Freud's most incisive, if dense, discussion of this closed economy of libidinal energy is found in "Instincts and Their Vicissitudes" (1915), in *The Standard Edition of the Complete Psychological Works of Sigmund Freud,* vol. 14, ed. James Strachey in collaboration with Anna Freud (London: Hogarth, 1964), 110-40.

28. Foucault, *Discipline and Punish,* 28.

29. Ibid., 29.

30. Ibid.

31. Ibid.

32. The focus on the relationship between exteriority and interiority is highlighted in one element of Gilles Deleuze's reading of Foucault. See *Foucault,* trans. and ed. Sèan Hand, foreword Paul Bovè (Minneapolis: University of Minnesota Press, 1988), "Strategies or the Non-stratified: The Thought of the Outside (Power)," 70-93, and "Foldings, or the Inside of Thought (Subjectification)," 94-123.

33. Foucault, *Discipline and Punish,* 23.

34. Here I paraphrase loosely from Thomas Hobbes, *Leviathan,* ed. C. B. MacPherson (New York: Penguin, 1968).

35. See "Two Lectures," in Michel Foucault, *Power\Knowledge: Selected Essays and Interviews, 1972-77,* ed. Colin Gordon, trans. Colin Gordon, Leo Marshall, John Mepham, and Kate Soper (New York: Pantheon, 1980), 97-8.

36. Ibid., 106.

37. For a prime example of how liberals approach the issue of cruelty see Shklar, *Ordinary Vices.* For a critique, see Dumm, *united states.* William E. Connolly presents a critique of liberalism that similarly develops this Foucaultian insight. See his *Identity\Difference: Democratic Negotiations of Political Paradox* (Ithaca, NY: Cornell University Press, 1991).

38. For a full treatment of this dimension of the modern self, see Wikse, *About Possession.*

39. Foucault, *Discipline and Punish,* 47.

40. Ibid., 49.

41. Ibid., 50.

42. Ibid., 45.

43. Ibid., 51.

44. Ibid., 53.

45. Ibid., 56.

46. Ibid., 58.

47. Ibid., 63.

48. Ibid., 69.

49. Ibid., 74.

50. Ibid., 77.

51. Ibid., 78.

52. Ibid., 79.

53. Ibid., 80.

54. Ibid., 82.

55. Ibid.

56. Ibid., 85.

57. Ibid., 87.

58. Ibid., 88. In this analysis, Foucault is close to being in agreement with the celebrated neo-Marxian analysis of the transition to the modern age outlined by Barrington Moore, Jr. See *Social Origins of Dictatorship and Democracy: Lord and Peasant in the Making of the*

Modern World (Boston: Beacon Press, 1966), Part One, "Revolutionary Origins of Captialist Democracy."

59. Ibid., Foucault, *Discipline and Punish,* 87.

60. For an analysis of how this sort of operation worked in the context of English colonialism, see Thomas L. Dumm, *Democracy and Punishment: Disciplinary Origins of the United States* (Madison, University of Wisconsin Press, 1987), especially Chapter 3.

61. Ibid., 93.

62. Ibid., 128.

63. Ibid., 131.

64 For a more detailed discussion of the emergence of discipline that thinks about it as the underbelly of constitutionalism, see op. cit., *Democracy and Punishment,* especially Chapter 4.

65. For a discussion of the function of prisons as a means of controlling and monitoring the flow of unattached men in colonial and postcolonial North America, see David Rothman, *The Discovery of the Asylum* (Boston: Little, Brown, 1971).

66. This body remains gendered a male body, although as discipline extends its reach the tools of power associated with it extend to encompass the female body and other bodies as well. The differentiations of power as it constitutes the male and female subject, and as theorized by Foucault, have been the source of an extraordinarily fecund scholarship in feminist political theory, although most directly this scholarship has emerged in connection as a consequence of readings of Foucault's *The History of Sexuality.*

67. Foucault, *Discipline and Punish,* 138.

68. Ibid., 141-5.

69. Ibid., 149-54.

70. Ibid., 160.

71. Ibid., 163-4.

72. Ibid., 169.

73. Ibid., 177.

74. Ibid., 183.

75. See Thomas L. Dumm, "Fear of Law," in *Studies in Law and Society* (London: JAI, 1990).

76. In this observation, I both rely upon and depart from the reading of Foucault rendered so persuasively by Diane Rubenstein. See her "Food for Thought: Metonymy in the Late Foucault," in James Bernauer and David Rasmussen, eds., *The Final Foucault* (Cambridge: MIT Press, 1988), 83-101. Rubenstein concentrates her efforts on describing the metonymic displacements from *Discipline and Punish* through the succceeding volumes of *The History of Sexuality.* See especially pp. 88-9. I seek to monitor both these displacements to which Rubenstein draws attention, but also to see them as they occur within the texts as well.

77. I write this parenthetical note from the friendly confines of Amherst College, one of whose founding trustees was the first major American lexicographer, Noah Webster.

78. Foucault, *Discipline and Punish,* 160.

79. Ibid., 194.

80. Ibid., 224.

81. Michel Foucault, "Of Other Spaces," trans. Jay Misoweic, *diacritics,* Spring 1986, 27.

82. Ibid., 23.

83. The issue of space in Foucault's work is most prominently addressed in Edward Soja, *Postmodern Geographies: The Reassertion of Space in Critical Social Theory* (London: Verso,

1989), 16-21. Also see Dumm, "Fear of Law." I address the question of space in Foucault's thought more systematically in Chapter 2.

84. Foucault, *Discipline and Punish,* 200.

85. Ibid., 204.

86. Ibid., 206-7.

87. Ibid., 208.

88. Foucault, "Of Other Spaces," 24. I mention this as a too brief response to the critique of Foucault that has been inspired by Gayatri Spivak's intervention, "Can the Subaltern Speak?" in Lawrence Grossberg, ed., *Reinterpreting Marxism* (Urbana: University of Illinois Press, 1989). Spivak's essay has been seized upon by old guard New Leftists to dismiss poststructuralism generally and genealogical approaches to issues of politics specifically. See, for instance, an essay by Neil Lazarus, "Postmodernism and Global Culture," *Differences,* 3, no. 3 (Fall 1991): 94-138. Lazarus presumes that a simple privileged subject position afflicts Foucault, making him not interested in the most important matters of oppression. One would guess that Lazarus is merely ignorant of Foucault's political biography, his intense activism, and the documented acts of his personal courage, but that ignorance only makes such personal condemnations more repulsive.

89. Foucault, *Discipline and Punish,* 202.

90. Foucault, "Of Other Spaces," 26.

91. Foucault, *Discipline and Punish,* 207. Foucault is quoting from Bentham's plan for a Panopticon. See Jeremy Bentham, *Works,* vol. 4, ed. John Bowring (Edinburgh: London, Simpkin, Marshall, 1843), 39.

92. Foucault, *Discipline and Punish,* 222.

93. Ibid., 227-8.

94. Ibid., 249.

95. Ibid., 248.

96. Ibid., 251.

97. Ibid., 254.

98. Ibid., 255.

99. Ibid., 256.

100. The anarchistic elements of Foucault's thinking about freedom are explored most sympathetically by John Rajchman, *Michael Foucault: The Freedom of Philosophy* (New York: Columbia University Press, 1985), and Todd May, *The Political Philosophy of Post-structuralist Anarchism* (University Park: Pennsylvania State University Press, 1994).

101. Foucault, *Discipline and Punish,* 268.

102. Ibid., 281.

103. Much of my interpretation of the role of the vagabonds in *Discipline and Punish* depends in part on an earlier reading of this passage by Alexander E. Hooke. See "The Order of Others: Is Foucault's Antihumanism Against Human Action?" *Political Theory* 15, no. 1 (February 1987): 38-60.

104. Foucault, *Discipline and Punish,* 290.

105. Ibid.

106. Deleuze, *Foucault,* 42.

107. Ibid., 43.

108. On the politics of fear, see Dumm, *Democracy and Punishment,* "Conclusion: From Danger to Fear."

109. Foucault, *Discipline and Punish,* 296.

4

Freedom and Seduction

Does the expression "let us liberate our sexuality" have a meaning? Isn't the problem rather to try to decide the practices of freedom through which we could determine what is sexual pleasure and what are our erotic, loving, passionate relationships with others? It seems to me that to use this ethical problem of the definition of practices of freedom is more important than the affirmation (and repetitious, at that) that sexuality and desire must be set free.

—"The Ethic of the Care for the
Self as a Practice of Freedom"

C ould it be that the great project of disciplinary society is coming to an end? What would it mean to see the end of a project that has resulted in the emergence of a civilization constituted by the practices that made bodies useful, that imposed upon them rituals of truth

Epigraph taken from "The Ethic of the Care for the Self as a Practice of Freedom," in James Bernauer and David Rasmussen, eds., *The Final Foucault* (Cambridge: MIT Press), 3.

and established a particular regime of power that has sustained itself for two centuries now? We might think about the displacements implied by the possibility of the end of disciplinary society. A utopian version of this end is anticipated in Marxian speculations concerning the demise of capitalism, speculations that have envisioned the emergence of a true species-being as the accompaniment of the release from disciplined labor under capital and the withering away of the state. The flourishing of all sorts of possibilities and liberations of being are imagined to accompany the revolution. The implicit premise of such utopian possibilities is the promise of some sort of complete freedom. If we followed the utopian premise we might understand freedom to be the removal of constraints on the activities of people, who would be able to behave otherwise in the absence of repression. Freedom would be available to all people through the relaxation and eventual elimination of the forces that would constrain it. But this vision of freedom has never comprehended the constitutive powers that situate it. In understanding freedom to be the opposite of repression, utopian thinkers misapprehend the positive, constitutive character of power as it operates in shaping how we are free, as Foucault demonstrates in *Discipline and Punish.* The idea that an end of disciplinary society would result in freedom as liberation thus remains a chimera.

In *Discipline and Punish,* Foucault suggests that he is writing a history of the present. We might know this history as having as its subject the disciplinary form our freedom has taken. The symbol of disciplinary society, what Foucault calls its exemplary institution, is Bentham's Panopticon. Since Foucault's elevation of Bentham's invention in *Discipline and Punish,* panopticism has come to stand not only for the technique by which discipline would be disseminated throughout society but as a shorthand for both the character of the penitentiary itself and the regimented qualities of mass society. Hence, one reading of the role of the contemporary penitentiary—a very tempting one in that it merely asks that we extrapolate the present into the indefinite future—is that it remains a primary site and major generator of discipline. From this perspective, the intense growth of penal systems and populations within them and the emergence of secondary disciplinary systems such as parole directly correspond to an intense extension of discipline throughout contemporary society. One might then argue that the modern penitentiary has reached such iconic and practical significance that an ordered society has become unimaginable without it.

In the United States in particular, if one took at face value the resurgence in the rhetoric and evolution of policy initiatives toward the need to restore morality and imprison those who violate law, the disciplinary project would seem to be in greater ascendance than at any time in this country's history. In this era of great state frugality, the largest growth in governmental spending at both the federal and state levels in the United States is for prison construction. The United States holds a record number of prisoners in confinement, second only to Russia on a per capita basis, and given the general collapse of political authority in Russia one might wonder if there is not a parallel collapse taking place in the United States. Moreover, there may have been an intensification of the prison project in recent years, in that policy makers lean ever more heavily on its form and substance as an instrument of policy. Contemporarily, the prison is coming to operate as a replacement institution for schools (the treatment of juveniles as adults for purposes of criminal trial criminalizes delinquency rather than "delinquent-izing" criminality), for mental hospitals (the gradual abandonment of the utility of the insanity plea has led to the execution of people who formerly would be considered criminally insane), for barracks (the option, popular in an earlier era, of entering the military as a judicially recommended way of avoiding trial for crimes has disappeared, although "boot camps" for young criminal offenders are becoming popular), and for factories (in a post-industrial society, the discipline of labor is an anachronism), all of which once resembled prisons.[1]

In short, if disciplinary society is in decline, why do we have so many prisons? We might ask in response, what would become of this penitentiary if discipline was in decline? The continued existence of prisons and their expansion should not mislead us: penitentiary buildings do not need to be demolished if they are no longer to operate as penitentiaries. They merely need to cease to function as sites for the inculcation of discipline. Their relationship to discipline might dissolve, and yet they could remain standing. If this happened, new uses might be found for them. Prison would become a substitute, but a substitute for what? It would become a substitute for the penitentiary itself and would take its place in the new order as an ancillary institution to the shape of postdisciplinary power. The examples from this century are not encouraging. Internment camps, modern penal colonies, intensely monitored ghettos, segregated "homelands," and the systematic destruction of categories of people, or what is usually called genocide, can all be thought of as replacements of the penitentiary.

Unfortunately, we do not need to qualify what is happening. The irony of contemporary punishment derives from the very fact that the penitentiary has ceased to function as such. Prisons are now a site from which a disassembling of the discipline once inculcated within them is taking place. In the United States, which remains an exemplary place of freedom, we are witnessing or participating in—depending on the support we provide for the expansion of prisons and the punitive criminal policies that feed them—a perverse reversal, one that seems to be uncannily temporal as well as substantive, as the forces that have organized normalized society become undone. The reversal itself is reflected in such strange innovations in the juridical system as the return of the chain gang, a renewed hunger for capital punishment, and a general consensus that prisons should be places of misery for those who offend the law.

But it would also be a mistake to understand the demise of the penitentiary simply as a recrudescence of the old style of punishment. The reversal we are witnessing occurs in a context quite different from that of the rise of discipline. Then, bodies needed to be made useful. Now, the triumph of normalizing strategies has reconfigured the field of reality against which the play of power occurs. Instead of giving rise to expressions of concern about disorder, corruption, and the continued need to manage criminal populations in such a way as to provide guidance to the rest of a more docile citizenry, the indiscipline of prisons and jails and the violent crime on the streets of urban centers are popularly comprehended now as the ordinary conditions of an entire population of people. Punishment is currently a condition applauded or acquiesced to by those outside of the confines of prisons, and there is little expression of concern about the systemic corruptions of criminal prosecution, or the conditions within prisons themselves.[2] In fact, a disturbing implicit agreement by the citizenry of the United States seems to have been enacted over the past decade. Prisons are overcrowded and underfunded; there are levels of cruelty and danger within prisons that are encouraged by those who administer them. These are simple facts amply documented in prison literature.[3] We all agree that such conditions exist, but we continue to complain about there being too many rights for criminals, thereby endorsing the official story of formal rights and tacitly acknowledging the cruelty of prison life.

At the level of what we might call governmental ideology, the intense focus on issues of criminality as a political issue is accompanied by the rise in popularity of a new idea concerning the meaning of freedom. Freedom has become a synonym for personal security. To be secure is now understood by governmental authorities to be the first freedom, that is, the freedom from which all other freedoms flow and are made possible.[4] Yet this ideology of freedom contains within it discordant elements. Most people acknowledge that life within the confines of enclosed housing developments, behind banks of security monitors, with identification cards and bar codes ensuring access to particular spaces of freedom, has the general tenor of being a confinement, indeed, operates as a form of confinement. So the delinquent—whose habitat is outside the new enclosures of the privileged—is now acknowledged by some to be a symbol of freedom.[5] The prison may well be becoming the depository of practical freedom in an age when the practice of freedom is to be understood as the antimony of security, even as security itself operates as a sign of the ideal of freedom. Hence, the expansion of the prison might be understood as a sign of a greater confinement of the possibility of being free. If this is the case, then in the neglected chambers of the prisons, in the hidden places of abjection that have ceased to be penitentiaries and have become places of concentration instead, the exercise of freedom continues to evolve. If this is so, we need to ask: What forms of the governance of the self are emerging as discipline itself becomes more rare? What ethics of governance might we anticipate emerging from the conjunctions of new heterotopias?

I do not maintain lightly that we are at the end of the era of discipline. To do so would be to suggest that the dysfunctions of contemporary society associated with the social chaos and strife presumably caused by economic, political, and geodemographic dislocations are effects of causes larger than themselves, associated with an immense transformation of life for the inhabitants of the West and, given the West's domination of world resources and its hegemony over the world's rituals of truth, for the world as a whole. But this is indeed the risk that Foucault believes we face. Because discipline focuses on a set of practices designed to call a self into being, it brings into existence a self to be governed. After the establishment of such a self, the general de-emphasis on disciplinary practices comes to be reflected in both an increase in the individual *incapacity* to be self-ruled and the increasing commodification of discipline itself: discipline becomes a rarified value, available through regulated dispersal to those who are to manage the systems of postdisciplinary normalization. Why and how does this shift occur?

Normalization/Government/Security

In the first volume of *The History of Sexuality* (*The Will to Truth*), Foucault connects the rise of normalization (with which he concludes *Discipline and Punish*) with a biopolitics that puts entire populations at risk. In the final essay in that volume, "Right of Death and Power Over Life," he examines "sexuality" as a field of power. Sexuality is a primary site where both the formation of a confessing subject and the establishment of the strategies that would enable the control of populations are conjoined as "two poles of development linked together by a whole intermediary cluster of relations."[6] He argues that the sovereign right to decide life and death has undergone a profound transformation, one consistent with the transformation in the overall logic of power. Power was once the "right of seizure: of things, time, bodies, and ultimately life itself; it culminated in the privilege to seize hold of life in order to suppress it."[7] But this power of seizure is but one element in the modern repertoire of power. The form of power in the modern era is, as Foucault explained in *Discipline and Punish,* "a power bent on generating forces, making them grow, and ordering them, rather than one dedicated to impeding them, making them submit, or destroying them."[8] The paradox is that this exercise of a life-sustaining power occurs during the era that has been witness to the unleashing of the most formidable powers of death in human history.

> But this formidable power of death—and this is perhaps what accounts for part of its force and the cynicism with which it has so greatly expanded its limits—now presents itself as the counterpart of a power that exerts a positive influence on life, that endeavors to administer, optimize, and multiply it, subjecting it to precise controls and comprehensive regulation. Wars are no longer waged in the name of a sovereign who must be defended; they are waged on behalf of the existence of everyone; entire populations are mobilized for the purpose of wholesale slaughter in the name of life necessity; massacres have become vital.[9]

For Foucault, the principles of battle are now attached to the survival strategies of states. These survival strategies of bio-power, which operate at both the macro level of populations and the micro level of sexualities, have raised the stakes of politics to a new high. The continued existence of a sovereignty no longer is the final arbitrator of how far power will be exercised; instead, the stakes of power are raised to risk the biological existence of an entire population in the name of its continued survival. Foucault writes, "If genocide is indeed the dream of modern powers, this is not because of a recent return of the ancient right to kill; it is because power is situated and exercised at the level of life, the species, the race, the large-scale phenomena of population."[10] In short, Foucault argues, the right of the sovereign to take life or let live has been replaced by "a power to *foster* life or *disallow* it to the point of death."[11]

The disciplines explained by Foucault in his earlier work constitute one pole of the exercise of this power. What he calls "the bio-politics of the population" constitutes the other. This latter area concerns problems of birth rate, migration, and public health. It involves the emergence of demography and the economic instrumentalization of the modern state. Of course, these two arenas of power combine. But for Foucault, the emergence of the two poles of power most importantly means not the emergence of a new ascetic morality but "nothing less than the entry of life into history, that is, the entry of phenomena peculiar to the life of the human species into the order of knowledge and power, into the sphere of political techniques."[12] This development means that although in some ways the issue of death has receded from human concern since the eighteenth century, since there has emerged a relative control over it, the very distance from death paradoxically has given humankind the leverage to put it at greater risk. We have become, during the modern era, a species that is collectively more aware of its *aliveness* than ever before. This development has meant that the stakes of power simply must be raised to a level commensurate with its object; power has had to express itself at the level of life itself. Foucault summarizes this matter in terms that underline the perils we face:

It is not that life has been totally integrated into techniques that govern and administer it; it constantly escapes them. Outside the Western world, famine exists, on a greater scale than ever; and the biological risks confronting the species are perhaps greater, and certainly more serious, than before the birth of microbiology. But what be called a society's "threshold of modernity" has been reached when the life of the species is wagered on its own political strategies. For millennia, man remained what he was for Aristotle: a living animal with the additional capacity for a political existence; modern man is an animal whose politics places his existence as a living being in question.[13]

In other words, the political situation of the modern era is unique in regard to the threat that its form constitutes to human life itself.[14]

One might think that this effect is contained by the politics of interstate conflict, but Foucault's point is precisely the opposite. In the growing importance of the norm Foucault identifies the dissolution of the sovereign boundaries established by law. These boundaries have been underwritten by the power of the sword. The dynamic of their dissolution encouraged the emergence of the modern state as the focal point of governance even as it ensured that the hegemony of the state would always be contestable. For Foucault, such a power is no longer the primary effective site of politics because the regulatory and corrective mechanisms for the administration of life are much more attuned to strategies of normalization than they are to the power of prohibition. The form of law remains in place, but the law comes to act more and more as a norm. Judicial institutions are retrofitted, as it were, into a set of institutions designed to place subjects within the normalized order.[15] As Foucault states, "A normalizing society is the historical outcome of a technology of power centered on life."[16] Moreover, to presume that there is an opposition between normalizing strategies and the establishment of modern rights through the creation of constitutions is mistaken. "We should not be deceived by all the Constitutions framed throughout the world since the French Revolution, the Codes written and revised, a whole continual and clamorous legislative activity: these were the forms that made an essentially normalizing power acceptable."[17] In the emergence of disciplinary society rights themselves become decoupled from the power of sovereignty.

The "right" to life, to one's body, to health, to happiness, to the satisfaction of needs, and beyond all the oppressions or "alienations," the "right" to re-discover what one is and all that one can be, this "right"—which the classical juridical system was utterly incapable of comprehending—was the political response to all these new procedures of power which did not derive, either, from the traditional right of sovereignty.[18]

The establishment of a new right—"to rediscover what one is"—gradually comes about at first slowly and then suddenly, this post-sovereign right becomes decoupled from discipline. The emergence of this new, non-disciplinary, nonsovereign right can be seen as a response to Foucault's own demand for a new form of power that would avoid the "blind alley" of the confrontation between sovereignty and discipline. From his perspective, the idea that there is actually a confrontation between sovereignty and discipline is ultimately false. The two elemental foci of power do not oppose but complement each other by constituting the field through which the governance of life through normalization can occur.[19] The practice of normalization in the wake of discipline lends itself to the struggle to find ways of being that will enable modern subjects to confront the establishment of themselves as normal beings. It does so by engaging in a kind of retreat from the details of governance.

Normalization, as it becomes decoupled from disciplinary practices, issues in governance at a distance. In fact, Foucault himself suggests that the most important form of control in such a system of governance is achieved by apparatuses of security.[20] This shift—from the dominance of apparatuses of discipline to that of apparatuses of security—occurs within the realm of normalization. Its most significant effect on practices of freedom has to do with a de-emphasis on the inculcation of individualizing discipline and a new emphasis on the mass control of elements of behavior. Normalization as a strategy of security permits a withdrawal from the special interventions of discipline by striving to control populations at large through monitoring, surveys, and other indirect methods of identifying and establishing norms of behavior. Through the establishment of norms, people become elements of systems of equivalence that substitute, for an individuality constituted through disciplinary practices, a community of security based upon comparisons to a standard based upon an average. Because no single person is ever average, no one is ever completely normal. One's place within the confines of such a system is determined by the attributes one shares with others. Each attribute places a dimension of an individual's life on a specific continuum of meaning. But personhood itself is fragmented, and elements of it become signs of one's place in reference to a specific norm.[21] Security as a dominant technique of governance operates successfully precisely to the extent that no person can be assured of being secure.

In this framework, security comes to supersede freedom, initially by establishing freedom as a constantly deferred good achievable only after the grounds of its practice are adequately established. And because the strategies of normalization that operate in reference to security are not designed to establish such grounds, freedom, understood here in terms of being a possession, is itself never secured. Instead, the discourse of freedom as security allows for there to be a strategic use of the rhetoric of freedom to intensify control over populations at large. The spatial configurations that seemed to establish the divisions that would allow for freedom to exist are undermined by the imperative for security. They become virtual shadows of their former selves, illusions even unto themselves, and everyone is exposed to the powers of intensified normalizing practices. The securing of self is more and more closely tied to participation in or acknowledgment of one's desituated place on the (largely) demographically and economically determined scales of meaning.

We can see the paradox of securing freedom demonstrated in a review of the recent debates concerning crime and its connection to security in the United States. In November 1993, President Clinton met at the White House with a group of academics (a meeting organized by William Galston, a communitarian political theorist serving as a domestic advisor to the Clinton administration) for the express purpose of reflecting on his first year in office. Among the visitors was Michael Sandel of Harvard, whose comments apparently generated the most interest. Sidney Blumenthal reports,

> Sandel urged [the President] to step back from details of policy to articulate broader purposes. He should connect his Presidency with the moral aspirations of Americans, in order to change the terms of the political discourse. Conservatives had made a monopoly of claims on the moral dimension, but Clinton had to recapture it for progressive ends. He had to speak to the widespread sense that people's lives are out of control and that they feel a loss of community. An urgency about restoring meaning to civic life could come from dealing with crime and violence. As Sandel spoke, the President asked a White House usher to get him a pen, and he took notes on the back of the dinner menu.[22]

We might note that the primary symptoms of the withdrawal of discipline are summarized in Sandel's argument—a lack of meaning, a loss of control, a feeling of the loss of community. These are to be addressed by a restoration of security through "dealing with" crime and violence. Crime and violence operate as both demonological symbols of lack of security and as a residual site, a hidden historical reminder of the function the penitentiary once served as an inculcator of discipline.

Shortly after this meeting President Clinton opened a major initiative to intensify sanctions against crime by subtly attacking the old regime of rights. Citing Martin Luther King, Jr. as an example, Clinton argued that were he alive in the 1990s King would have said, " 'I did not fight for the right of black people to kill each other with reckless abandon.' "[23] And in an interview following that speech, Clinton indicated that he understood how the issue of criminality stood in for the entire complex of issues facing a postdisciplinary society:

> Pretty soon you have to face the whole issue of the implications of the family breakdown and the economic collapse in many of these areas, and whether the schools are functioning properly, and why there are no jobs for these folks. But if you start with this core of common values and the desire of people to be secure in their homes, their persons, and their lives, and to see children brought up in safety, you can work that back to a lot of these other issues in ways that break them out of their little boxes in their minds—the liberal/ conservative boxes, or their Democrat / Republican boxes, or their government/ private sector boxes. . . . And what struck me was that without a certain amount of *security* people's lives are not ordered enough and they are not personally self-confident enough to undertake the changes necessary to triumph in the world we're living in, in the world toward which we are moving. Because we are living in an environment of permanent, sweeping change. Security is usually something that is positioned against change, you know?[24]

The diagnosis Clinton presents here is consistent with Foucault's analysis of governmentality. It focuses on the capacities of power to order across the boundaries of family and economy, public sector and private sector. Clinton seeks to dedifferentiate the sites from which power is to be exercised and focuses instead on the effectiveness of the strategies themselves, noting the need for continued innovation in "an environment of permanent, sweeping change." (It is unclear whether Clinton means that the change is to have permanent effects or that constant change itself is to be the permanent condition of our era.) As a democratic leader, Clinton seeks to instruct the polity concerning its need to rethink security. Security must become as mobile as the forces that oppose it.

Locating crime policy within a matrix of issues concerning the dynamics of social transformation and the hunger for protection is, perhaps, the most obvious political dimension of contemporary communitarianism. Sandel, who I would suggest is the contemporary communitarian political theorist most carefully attuned to the dangerous consequences of his position for the practice of freedom, comes closest to disclosing the connection between this element of desire for security and the anxieties created by constant flux. In an essay in which he develops a political strategy for Democrats in response to the moralisms of the Republicans, Sandel argues that American liberalism has been compulsively individualistic and lacks a "second voice," that of community. Republicans, though, have not made the same error. For Sandel, the most important element of Ronald Reagan's success in transforming American political discourse stemmed from his appeal to communal, traditionalist, and Christian fundamentalist elements that articulate, however inadequately, this second voice. For Sandel, "there is nothing intrinsically conservative about family or neighborhood or community or religion. To the contrary, under modern conditions, traditional values cannot be vindicated by conservative policies."[25] Sandel is able to claim that such institutions are not intrinsically conservative only by overlooking major features of them. To argue, for instance, that religion is not intrinsically conservative requires that one examine only the explicit pieties embraced by religions and not the ancillary role that religions play in support of reactive powers through the renunciations they impose upon believers and the incitements they provoke against those who live outside or on the margins of their communities. For Sandel, though, these implicit undertones of various religions (and one might identify similar undertones in the other two institutions he endorses) are less important than the fact that they exist as pregiven elements in a strategy that enables there to be a positive governmental intervention in the establishment of local control over morality. He reads contemporary American government as being morally incapacitated by what he sees as its liberal neutrality, an inability to fill a moral vacuum in the lives of citizens. As he argues, "A public life empty of moral meanings and shared ideals does not secure freedom but offers an open invitation to intolerance."[26]

Sandel wants to "secure freedom." This phrase echoes a passage from the American Declaration of Independence—to "secure these rights." But the imperative to achieve the security of freedom itself can be seen as the culmination of the developments associated with the decoupling of rights from the power of sovereignty, as Foucault suggests. Sandel's desire to fill a moral vacuum presumes that this vacuum itself is a result of a particular way of managing the modern economy, a rift in the otherwise stable set of moral conventions that govern life, including religion, family and neighborhood. To the extent that there is a destabilizing force for communitarians, it is liberalism, which communitarians see as having succeeded in creating a "public life empty of moral meanings" in its establishment of a "neutral space" of the public sphere.

But Foucault understands that the constitution of liberal rights is complementary to the establishment of discipline: it is not simply the management of the modern economy that is at stake but the much broader transformation of the Western world into a civilization of productivity. The communitarian hunger to secure a space for freedom by filling this liberal sphere of freedom with a pregiven set of values coincides with the need of a postdisciplinary normalizing society, establishing criteria against which deviance can be identified and marginalized through strategies that deindividualize the subjects of power. Advanced techniques of monitoring enforce normalization without recourse to individuating discipline, and in so doing they also automatically operate to marginalize those who do not come close to the statistical norm.[27] The values that constitute normality do not depend on the disciplining of individuals but, instead, on the identification and cultivation of common experiences beyond individual religious belief, family bond, or local loyalty. This evocation of common experience is the substance of the political rationality of governmentality in the late modern era. Instead of a retrieval of values, older values are simulated: simulated belief in God, simulated nuclear families, simulated communities all serve as markers of reassurance to people who seem otherwise left bereft of a sense of meaning in their lives. This strategy of governance through normalization should not be confused with a return to traditional values. But communitarians pretend that in fact it is possible to go back to a premodern condition, accompanied by the amenities provided by the very techniques, disciplinary strategies and normalizing practices that prevent that step from ever being taken. What communitarians really want to secure is not freedom but *stable identities* for themselves and, as a necessary correlative, for those who can safely be labeled "others." The practices they endorse are all normalizing ones, all designed to identify the criteria around which normalized identities can be named, even though such identities cannot ever be stabilized. They seek claims to identity that will not need constant renegotiation. They seek, in short, the sort of governance that will curtail practices of freedom in the name of security.

Communitarians are not alone in their drive to reestablish order through a return to values that antedate the modern era. One might in fact see the resurgence of various fundamentalisms throughout the world to be the most salient symptom of the anxieties afflicting a world civilization now commonly shaped by the power of normalization. Indeed, the new Manicheanism that seeks to divide this world into good and evil and insists upon a purity of identity on both sides of the equation participates in the intensification of normalizing activity, allowing there to be an upping of the ante in regard to the risks that populations are to undergo in the name of sovereign communities. Casting blame for evil in every outward direction, contemporary fundamentalists are remarkably adept at avoiding a confrontation with another major source of evil: their own desire to impose order on others is so intense that it contributes to the obliteration of others through both its metaphysical and physical incitements to violence.[28]

Foucault enables us to see in such desires the workings of the complex identities and identifications through which modern differences are contested and negotiated.[29] How are we to negotiate identity without falling into the trap of strong identification? Resorting to the moral philosophies that depend upon the strong identifications of the past is doomed to reinforce the normalizing kind of power relationships that have enlisted life itself. Against the tendency to reinforce normalizing power Foucault presents an elusive strategy, one not designed to reassert an order of things over and above the present structure of power but, instead, to allow for the possibilities of a deintensification of the fields of subjectivity that hold us in place. This strategy is one of resistance. The pressures at work to hold subjects in place have become more intense as earlier techniques for doing so by holding them together—religious belief, subsistence economies, the sexual division of labor and discipline itself, to name some important ones—have become obsolete. Normalization appears as a simplification of these techniques, the cynical remainder of what was formerly reinforced by belief. To find new ways to negotiate the constitution of self that resist the normalizing powers of the present without falling into the trap of former beliefs is a simple way of describing Foucault's ethical project.

Ethics

What is the alternative to this recursive effort to "fill the vacuum," that is, to endorse those conventional moralities that do little more than operate to intensify the disparities established by normalization as it moves into the field of the life processes themselves? Georges Canguilhem, in a provocative note, suggests that the "final" Foucault, the Foucault concerned with the elaboration of an ethics, is the inevitable result of his own insights into the field of normalization. Canguilhem writes,

> It seems in fact that the effort sustained in order to track down every surreptitious enterprise of normalization under the appearance of the sole "authority" of knowledge is the sign, in the work of Foucault, of a profound personal refusal to offer himself as a model, to produce himself as a master .... Is it understandable from this why what could be taken as a rupture in the last works of Michel Foucault would only be at its core a completion precipitated, perhaps, by a premonitory anxiety? It was normal, in the properly axiological sense, that Foucault would undertake the elaboration of an ethics. In the face of normalization and against it, *Le Souci de soi.*[30]

In Canguilhem's reading, the care of the self emerges, not as a radically unsituated choice governing how to be, *pace* Sartre, but as an element in a series of resistances to the terms that have operated to define the self in reference to the pregiven identities of normalizing discourse. For him, Foucault responds to the radically desituating forces of normalization by elaborating an ethics. This simple declaration is very sensible, although we must also understand that for Foucault the ethical response does not carry with it the clarity of a code. Indeed, in the face of normalization, he suggests that we need to think for our selves, evading the demand for solutions. He does not ask how we might behave responsibly because that question has been superseded by normalizing discourse. "Behavior" itself should be understood for what it is, a reaction to the creation of a norm. He is instead concerned to ask how we might develop a care for the self that would enable one to become generous in our responses to others.

Foucault's turn to ancient Greece and Rome is inspired by the search for an ethos concerning the body that would not be associated with the renunciation of bodily being itself that is to be found in the sort of asceticism that he had already traced to the emergence of normalizing discourse. He suggests that the terms of the genesis and dissemination of the care of self were not to issue inevitably in the modern mode of asceticism associated with the development of the ethics of Christianity.[31] The last two volumes of *The History of Sexuality* are devoted to describing how he comes to his understanding of this other kind of care of self. He is able to show that Christianity made use of austere ethical sensibilities encouraged by Greco-Roman styles of the care of the self but that this relationship does not suggest that the latter moral code depends upon the earlier ethical sensibility. The codification encouraged by Christianity comes about through a more complicated process.[32] But instead of being implicated in the codification of morality, in the earlier period sexuality operated as a field through which a problematization of the self would issue forth in certain practices designed to encourage a particular aesthetic of existence that emphasized the play of restraint in the exercise of freedom.[33]

Of course, even at the level of their dissemination the ethics of ancient societies developed in a variety of different contexts that determined the different relationships to existence they would enjoy. As Foucault notes in what has been called his "final interview,"

> At first the morality of antiquity addressed itself only to a very small number of individuals; it did not require everybody to obey the same pattern of behavior. It concerned only a very small minority of people, even of the free people. There were several forms of freedom, and the freedom of the head of state or of the leader of the army had nothing to do with the freedom of the wise man. Then this morality expanded. At the time of Seneca or even more so at the time of Marcus Aurelius, it might have been valid for everybody, but there was never a question of making it an obligation for all. Morality was a matter of individual choice; anyone could come and share in it. . . . We are thus very far from the moral conformities, the structures of which are elaborated by sociologists and historians by appealing to a hypothetical average population.[34]

This distance is important in that it both gives us the capacity to examine a moral relationship to truth that differs from that which holds in our own era and allows us to see the elements of that relationship that are not totally disconnected from our time. Foucault suggests the sort of ad hoc procedure that ought to direct such a search, a way of retaining the capacity to problematize the relations to truth that bear upon each successive epoch.

> I believe that in this "fishing around" that one undertakes with the Greeks, one must absolutely not impose limits on oneself or establish in advance a sort of program which would allow one to say: this part of the Greeks I accept; this other part I reject. All of Greek experience can be taken up in nearly the same manner by each time taking into account differences of context, and by indicating the aspects of the experience that could perhaps be salvaged from the early period and those which could, on the contrary, be abandoned."[35]

The contexts that seems to count the most for Foucault are those in which the relationship of the self to truth is politicized through the body. This concern is at the heart of the project of *The History of Sexuality*. In explaining the shift in focus of the project from the first volume, Foucault suggests, "It was a matter of analyzing, not behaviors or ideas, nor societies and their 'ideologies,' but the *problematizations* through which being offers itself to be, necessarily, thought—and the *practices* on the basis of which these problematizations are formed."[36] Here is a reformulation of the task of *Discipline and Punish* and *The Will to Truth*. One can trace, through the care taken of bodies, the rituals of truth of a given era, not simply as the given contingencies of an era but as the practices through which the relationship of truth and freedom are problematized.

A crucially important problematization for Foucault has to do with the question of how the politics of the self came into being in early Western civilization. He pursues this question when he examines, most importantly, the exercise of freedom in relation to truth in his study of the relationship of ethics to politics, which he presents in his analysis of Plato's passages concerning Alcibiades.[37] Alcibiades is an ambitious man who seeks to dominate others. When he was younger, he refused to submit to the love of older men. Socrates declares his love for Alcibiades. Foucault suggests,

> [Socrates] will make Alcibiades submit, but in a different sense. They make a pact—Alcibiades will submit to his lover, Socrates, not in a physical but in a spiritual sense. The intersection of political ambition and philosophical love is "taking care of oneself."[38]

To *know* how to take care of himself, Alcibiades must *learn* how to take care of himself in the context of the political and erotic states of domination and submission. In the Socratic dialogue, taking care of oneself comes to be taking care of one's soul. In Foucault's reading, the care of the self thus is related to four main problems: politics and its relationship to the self, learning from others, concern with self and self-knowledge, and finally, care of self and philosophical love, the relation to a master.[39] Eventually, this care of self is to turn deeply inward, become something one undertakes for one's own sake and to provide a dimension of inner experience new to Western life. For Foucault, at the time of Socrates the care of the self operated as a moment of transition from an explicitly erotic and political intersection of domination to an internalized morality, or ethic of the self.

The relationship of freedom to truth that concerns Foucault in the end is that of *parrhesia,* an art of truth telling. The parrhesiast that he is most concerned to discuss in his last seminars is Socrates.[40] For Foucault, the parrhesiast is distinguished from other truth tellers precisely by his obligation to risk himself in the telling of a truth that concerns the present. He does so with the recognition that the truth of which he speaks must concern both himself and those to whom he speaks. Foucault understands that the self at risk in the Socratic dialogues is a fragile thing, one distant from the modern self who comes to be so deeply concerned to secure freedom in our present. Paradoxically, this ancient self becomes more recognizable to us in the works of the Stoics, who cultivated a self concerned with the matters of everyday life.[41] Although Foucault admires that self, he knows that it too is not to be a model for the present. Yet when Foucault urges us to free ourselves of ourselves, we might suspect that he is thinking of the aesthetics of self-fashioning that these Stoics concerned themselves to develop. They seized upon their practices in the context of slavery and saw their care of self as a form of inner freedom.

Although Foucault does not suggest that the inner freedom pursued by the Stoics is homologous with the freedom we pursue, when he turns back to the contemporary era he is better able to see how we exercise our freedom in the context of contemporary powers as *other than liberatory practices.* For he argues that even in the liberatory practices of colonized people,

> this act of liberation is not sufficient to establish the practices of liberty that later on will be necessary for this people, this society and these individuals to decide upon receivable and acceptable forms of their existence or political society. This is why I insist on the practices of freedom rather than on the processes which indeed have their place, but which by themselves, do not seem to me to be able to decide all the practical forms of liberty.[42]

The practice of freedom, he explains, is not opposed to power but is enabled by the presence of power. Conversely,

> One must observe also that there cannot be relations of power unless the subjects are free. If one or the other were completely at the disposition of the other and became his thing, an object on which he can exercise an infinite and unlimited violence, there would not be relations of power. In order to exercise a relation of power, there must be on both sides at least a certain form of liberty. . . . That means that in the relations of power, there is necessarily the possibility of resistance, for if there were no possibility of resistance—of violent resistance, of escape, of ruse, of strategies that reverse the situation— there would be no relations of power.[43]

This passage is a crucial rejoinder to the various political theorists who have dismissed Foucault's work as being totalizing, as providing a mono-lithic view of power that holds no possibility of freedom. It also is suggestive of the political character of the ethos of the care of the self. As he puts it, "To constitute one's self as a subject who governs implies that one has constituted himself as a subject having care for self."[44] Foucault does not want to see an end of power but, instead, wants to resituate power relations so that there would be a minimum of domination. In this way, we might take steps toward being able to recognize how we are free. But to act upon that understanding requires not only the adoption of appropriate rules but also an ethics, an ethos, a practice of self.[45]

This practice concerns itself with an easing of the tension between life and death, not in the name of a deathbound wish but in opposition to the struggle that has put us all at such great risk in the name of life.[46] The trans-gressive character of this practice is a consequence of the way in which transgression is the form that resistance takes against the claims of modern moralists. These moralists! They claim to be on the side of life against death, when it is their very insistence on this opposition that places so much of life itself at risk.

The play of power and freedom in the context of normalized society raises questions about the space of freedom we inhabit. By emphasizing the relationship of care of self with free practices of truth in ancient Greece and Rome, Foucault raises the issue of how we are to develop our own care. Does the space of freedom in a postdisciplinary society allow for the emergence of practices in which we might recognize ourselves as both politically and ethically efficacious beings? Foucault's investigation of the past provides him with a particular way of thinking about the renunciations we might make and the activities in which we might engage. How might we recognize the problems intrinsic to our present care of the self? How might we be ethical in the face of normalization? How might we, in short, engage in or develop a contemporary political ethos that does not fall into the trap engendered by the desire to secure identity? Foucault outlines the ethos we might follow in an essay that appeared after his death, "What Is Enlightenment?" One might consider that essay as an outline of the contemporary form that a care of the self might take. There he suggests how we might connect to the Enlightenment through "the permanent reactivation of an attitude—that is, of a philosophical ethos that could be described as a permanent critique of our historical era."[47]

The Enlightenment thus serves as the thematic of the modern age, the thought that gave rise to disciplinary society. Inspired by Baudelaire's attitude toward the modern, Foucault suggests that the adoption of the critical ethos responsive to Enlightenment entails both negative and positive commitments. Negatively, one must refuse "the 'blackmail' of Enlightenment," which for Foucault means that one must ignore those who insist that criticizing Enlightenment rationality is simply irrational and that one must be either for or against Enlightenment. The task of problematizing Enlightenment must, instead, entail an analysis of ourselves as beings who are historically determined, to a certain extent, by the Enlightenment but who eschew an essential orientation toward some "rational kernel" at the heart of the experience of Enlightenment. We must instead orient ourself toward "the contemporary limits of the necessary."[48] We also must not confuse Enlightenment with humanism, which is not an orientation toward the present but a set of themes designed to promote particular values and to provide a critical principle of differentiation between domains of conventionally understood terms of good and bad. Humanism itself is parasitical to conceptions of what it means to be human borrowed from religion, science, or politics. It operates as a justification, not as a critique. Hence it is opposed to Enlightenment.[49] Positively, the critical ethos Foucault endorses is a critical ontology of ourselves, characterized as a limit-attitude, through which we might investigate the question, "In what is given to us as universal, necessary, obligatory, what place is occupied by whatever is singular, contingent, and the product of arbitrary constraints? The point, in brief, is to transform the critique conducted in the form of a necessary limitation into a practical critique that takes the form of a possible transgression."[50] Criticism will no longer be transcendental but genealogical in design and archaeological in method.

> It will separate out, from the contingency that has made us what we are, the possibility of no longer being, doing, or thinking what we are, do, or think. It is not seeking to make possible a metaphysics that has finally become a science; it is seeking to give new impetus, as far and wide as possible, to the undefined work of freedom.[51]

Moreover, such criticism must be neither global nor radical, in the sense of seeking a total transformation of existence. Instead, the critical ontology of ourselves must adopt as its ethos "a historico-practical test of the limits that we may go beyond, and thus as work carried out by ourselves upon ourselves as free beings."[52]

Foucault understands that the critical practices he advocates are vulnerable to the accusation of quietism. His response is to suggest that there are ways of acknowledging the larger frameworks of power within which these critical practices occur that will bear upon the possibility of disconnecting capacities from the intensification of power relations. He emphasizes that he understands how these larger realms of practice are homogeneous in the conditions of their possibility, systematic at the level of the ways in which they contributed to how we are to be constituted as subjects of knowledge, power, and morals, and most generally, how these realms will always have an indeterminate bearing upon the recurrence of specific practices. "The study of modes of problematization (that is, of what is neither an anthropological constant nor a chronological variation) is thus the way to analyze questions of general import in their historically unique form."[53]

Rather than a quietism, some critics have come to understand Foucault's emphasis on contingency to result in a facile and easy mode through which a transformation of self can occur.[54] But Foucault understands not only that transformation is not easy but that it is illusory. For him, the critical ontology of ourselves is a way of practicing freedom that does not vacillate between the two poles of specific liberation and revolutionary transformation but, instead, operates as what might be called a situating force. By engaging in a critical ontology of ourselves, we engage in what Foucault calls "a patient labor giving form to our impatience for liberty."[55] Such a practice can enable us to generate ways of being free under conditions that would seem improbable at best, conditions that are themselves the results of the normalizing power of our time.

Freedom and Seduction

James Bernauer suggests that Foucault proposes a "post-Auschwitz ethic." "Foucault's ethics," he writes,

> proposes the wisdom of dispossession, not only of certain systems of thought and action but also of a muteness before our age's indigenous suffering. . . . Whereas the philosopher had once taught, through his own life, how death could be borne, he had come too often to teach in our age the superior wisdom of how to accept the massacre of others: in the name of truth. . . . The strategy of Foucault's resistance to this evil is an ethics for thought which consists in a series of questions whose pursuit manifests the assumption of ethical responsibility.[56]

Bernauer goes on to suggest that the famous statement by a guard at Auschwitz, "Hier ist kein warum" (Here there is no why), a statement embraced by many as the epigram for the experience of Auschwitz, can and must be resisted through an ethics that does, in fact, ask why, framing the "why" as a response to the pure moralities that seek to cast out from the realm of reasons the horror of extermination. Bernauer sees this questioning as an element in "the practice of an impure reason," the project Foucault proposed in "The Order of Discourse" as "an introduction into the very roots of thought of notions of chance, discontinuity, and materiality." Bernauer suggestively, if somewhat incoherently, argues first that "if philosophers have often conceived their task to be the harbouring of human existence from raw exposure to the contingent, Foucault tried to drive them back to sea" and then concludes by suggesting that "Foucault brought philosophy back to earth. The better to love it."[57]

Down to earth and out to sea—although Bernauer might seem confused in his geographical referents, his focus on sea and earth might better be understood as metaphors for infinity and finitude. The former registers as the need to recognize the contingent character of existence and the latter as the need to note existence's inevitable connection to limits. Foucault gestures toward the finitude of existence so that we might be relieved of the burden of the possibility of opening up experience infinitely, and he gestures toward its contingent character to give us hope even under the most extreme circumstances of constraint.

What of those circumstances of constraint? The Auschwitz guard who stated "Here there is no why" was speaking to Primo Levi,[58] whose memoir of his experience in Auschwitz might instruct us as an exemplar of how we might problematize the relationship of truth and freedom in our time. Levi tells his story by concentrating on the small details of everyday life in Auschwitz. He knows better than to make absolute statements, understanding that there is no commensurate experience against which one can test such statements. He writes,

> Sooner or later in life everyone discovers that perfect happiness is unrealizable, but there are few who pause to consider the antithesis: that perfect unhappiness is equally unattainable. The obstacles preventing the realization of both of these extreme states are of the same nature: they derive from our human condition which is opposed to everything infinite.[59]

For Levi this realization was a key to survival because it allowed the physical suffering imposed by existence in the camp to act as the scale, limiting what otherwise might have been a "void of despair." Levi's reasoning is consistent with Foucault: transformation is an illusion, the finitude of life suggests that we arrange ourselves in conformity to the partial shifts in circumstance that always lie under the arbitrary structures we have imposed upon them. Small details of quotidian life—how to wait in line for soup, learning the value of a spoon—become crucial. "We have learnt that everything is useful: the wire to tie up our shoes, the rags to wrap around our feet, waste paper to (illegally) pad out our jacket against the cold. . . . We have learnt, on the other hand, that everything can be stolen."[60]

In Auschwitz, the rules were so complicated and numerous that they were impossible to follow consistently. So one had to learn how to violate rules, according to a complex and informal protocol. The amount of food that one could acquire legally was not enough to sustain life. So one had to learn how to steal as a way of life. The standards of cleanliness were extraordinarily rigorous and yet filth was ubiquitous. So one had to learn how to act as though one could clean oneself. One had to try because one's ability to be human was deeply tied to one's habits. This lesson is imparted to Levi by another, older prisoner:

> that precisely because the Lager was a great machine to reduce us to beasts, we must not become beasts; that even in this place one can survive, to tell the story, to bear witness; and that to survive we must force ourselves to save at least the skeleton, the scaffolding, the form of civilization. We are slaves, deprived of every right, exposed to every insult, condemned to certain death, but we still possess one power, and we must defend it with all our strength for it is the last—the power to refuse our consent. . . . We must walk erect, without dragging our feet, not in homage to Prussian discipline but to remain alive, not to begin to die.[61]

The advice given Levi consists of maintaining discipline in order to allow the self to survive. The strategy of the Germans is to destroy the self-discipline of the prisoners, and in so doing begin the process of their physical destruction. The advice of the older prisoner is simple: if one is to evade the beginning of the process of dying, one must try to dodge the beginning of the *disallowance* of life. The disallowance of life begins by shattering the core identities of those who are constituted as the threat.[62] At the level of the operation of capillary powers, the embrace of discipline operates as a refusal, a form of resistance.

Routine both oppresses and helps. Levi notes that once one (if one) survives the initial disorienting shock of initiation, one might be able "to dig himself in, to secrete a shell, to build around himself a tenuous barrier of defence, even in apparently desperate circumstances."[63] Routine in such circumstances is a strange and shocking phenomenon when described to the outsider. Consider this simple description that Levi provides of the simple act of rising from bed in the morning. "When I have remade my bed and am dressed, I climb down on to the floor and put on my shoes. The sores on my feet reopen at once, and a new day begins."[64] The simple act of slipping into one's shoes is an occasion of pain, but this suffering can be contextualized, can be made into a marker of the routine of the day, and hence remind Levi of the finitude of his suffering. Survival in Auschwitz, then, involved a capacity to think in terms of finitude.

It also involved luck. That contingency played the most important role in Levi's survival is the first point he makes in his memoir. "It was my good fortune," he writes in the first sentence of his preface, "to be deported to Auschwitz only in 1944, that is, after the German government had decided, owing to the scarcity of labour, to lengthen the average lifespan of the prisoners destined for elimination."[65] One might read Levi's statement as an ironism, but it serves as a reminder that the forces outside the control of those subjected to power can sometimes determine their fortune. These forces may well be controlled by others (although the extent to which particular agents can be claimed as responsible for conditions is another question). That Levi's good fortune is contained within his larger misfortune is important, and his larger misfortune is coincidental to the emergence of genocide as a form of normalizing practice. This recognition of the essentially inessential character of his position makes it even harder to bear. Yet this recognition of the force of evil as a nonabsolute presence, with varying degrees of power over subjects, also relieves Levi of the need to renounce humanity in the name of justice. He is able to retain the human scale by coming to understand even the horrible evil of Nazi extermination in nonabsolute terms.

In the poem with which he begins his memoir, Levi demands that we "Consider if this is a man . . . . Who dies because of a yes or a no."[66] And if we don't? Levi curses those of us who will not "meditate that this came about." That he curses is telling because a curse is an act of willing that enlists contingency itself in its fulfillment. That his demand is that we meditate is as important. That meditation is the first action one should take, and the only demand that Levi makes, indicates his hope in the redemptive power of thought—but only to the extent that we also appreciate that the terms of thought are delimited by the very attempt to extinguish it, to create sites where there is no "why."

Within Auschwitz, there emerge different styles of survival, each one predicated on the combination of contingency, will, and the adaptative capacity developed by the individual prisoners in their previous lives. At the heart of Levi's memoir is a chapter entitled "The Drowned and the Saved," in which he describes varieties of survival and contrasts them with the experiences of those who do not have the capacity to survive.[67] The drowned are overcome by death before they can learn to live under the conditions of Auschwitz. In shock, weakened physically and emotionally, they cannot marshal the resources necessary to adapt to the routines that will give them a chance to live. "Their life is short, but their number is endless; they, the *Muselmänner,* the drowned, form the backbone of the camp, an anonymous mass, continually renewed and always identical, of non-men who march and labour in silence, the divine spark dead within them, already too empty to really suffer."[68] They have no story to tell because they all die—and die immediately. They are already dead, in a sense, upon arrival. They are in distinct contrast to the saved, who are various in style and substance, having been lucky in various ways, having hewn difficult and dangerous paths.

Levi is not very interested in the most common route to survival, becoming a "prominent."[69] Instead, he focuses on those who fight with their own strength to survive. "Survival without renunciation of any part of one's moral world—apart from powerful and direct interventions by fortune—was conceded only to very few superior individuals, made of the stuff of martyrs and saints."[70] Among these are inmates who engage in small acts of corruption, small and occasional expedients known as *kombinacje.* Stealing a broom, dancing to entertain civilian workers who will give some soup, operating in the black market economy as a cobbler— small acts allow such operators to get by.[71] Then there are people who through powerful self-discipline create the illusion of being powerful and thus become so. Such people separate themselves from others in order to gain the attention of higher authorities. But they do so not by being obsequious. On the contrary, they themselves condescend to others. They work hard, maintain a neat appearance even though the effort involves establishing "a regime of supplementary privations" in a context of great deprivations, all in the hope of being prepared when an opportunity for being picked from the ranks presents itself.[72] Yet another way of surviving is to be properly equipped, through prior environmental exposure and physical makeup, so as to be most suited to flourish in the environment of the death camp. Levi describes such a person as bestial, an atavism. Such a person "has survived the destruction from outside, because he is physically indestructible; he has resisted the annihilation from within because he is insane."[73]

These are three distinguishable kinds of survivor. We might note that each corresponds to a category of subjection that Foucault has identified. The *kombinacje* (named Schepschel) is a delinquent who survives by engaging in the tolerated illegalities of the dominant regime of power. The self-disciplined individual (named Alfred L.) is the most fitting survivor of the disciplinary regime of power. Because of his perfection of the role he is able to transfer to the higher ranks where disciplinary skills are still needed. The atavistic beast (named Elias) is for Levi someone actually suited to survive in a postdisciplinary world, where the coherence of self-discipline gives way to life without purpose. Levi asks, "Are there not all around us some Eliases, more or less in embryo? Do we not see individuals living without purpose, lacking all forms of self-control and conscience, who live not *in spite* of these defects, but like Elias precisely because of them?"[74] We might also note that none of these three categories reflects the ethos or ethics endorsed by Foucault, the ethics that I would like to think Levi embodies.

There is a fourth and final category of survivor of whom Levi speaks. He is exemplified by Henri, who "possesses a complete and organic theory on the way to survive in Lager. . . According to Henri's theory, there are three methods open to man to escape extermination which still allow him to retain the name of man: organization, pity, and theft."[75] Although Henri practices all three, what distinguishes him for Levi is how he uses pity. "There is no better strategist than Henri in seducing ('cultivating' he says) the English POWs," Levi explains.

> His instrument of penetration, with the English and with others, is pity. Henri has the delicate and subtly perverse body and face of Sodoma's San Sebastian: his eyes are deep and profound, he has no beard yet, he moves with a natural languid elegance. . . . Henri has discovered that pity, being a primary and instinctive sentiment, grows quite well if ably cultivated, particularly in the primitive minds of the brutes who command us, those very brutes who have no scruples about beating us up without a reason, or treading our faces into the ground; nor has the great practical importance of the discovery escaped him, and upon it he has built up his personal trade.[76]

Levi acknowledges that Henri is civilized, that talking with him is pleasant, that he feels warm and near, and that even affection with him seems possible. "One seems to glimpse, behind his uncommon personality, a human soul, sorrowful and aware of itself." Yet, for Levi, one can in the next moment glimpse something frightening, even diabolical, "hard and distant, enclosed in armour, the enemy of all, inhumanly cunning and

incomprehensible like the Serpent in Genesis."[77] Levi finds Henri disturbing, so disturbing that he states plainly, "I would give much to know his
life as a free man, but I do not want to see him again."[78]

Why? It is true that Henri is a seducer. Levi comes to sees his acts of
seduction as a reversal of the field of inhumanity—Henri uses those he
seduces and in his skill explicitly acknowledges the need to "cultivate"
those from whom he wants things. He instrumentalizes his subjectivity.
(Levi writes that he feels as though he has been "an instrument in his hands,"
p. 100.) He makes use of his physical attractiveness to get what he needs
to survive. But why is this so much more objectionable to Levi than the
other ways of surviving? What makes Levi compare him to the serpent
in Genesis?

One might think in terms of the dominant conventions of sexual
morality in the era of World War II. Henri as a seducer may well be equated
with Henri as a homosexual. In the context of Auschwitz this is almost
ludicrous—but only almost. The pink triangle is not mentioned by Levi at
any point in the book, although he labels Henri as being in possession of a
perverse body. A systematic destruction of the conventions through which
one had achieved one's preinstitutional sexual identity is surely part of the
power of Auschwitz: after all, it is part of the power of much lesser
postdisciplinary institutions of destruction such as the modern American
maximum security prison. Henri may have allowed these prisoners and
these Kapos to use his body for their sexual pleasure. More, he may have
made them want him, transmuting pity into desire. The degree of awareness
of others in higher positions that was required of Henri for him to enter
into seductive relationships may have also preyed upon Levi. After all, the
world of the POWs was of a different order than that of the *Häftling,* the
Jewish prisoners. Seduction itself then, might be understood to be a process
made visible in the flattened environment of thin selves, selves whose
resources have been diminished. It may be that the very transparency of
Henri's efforts disturbs Levi the most.[79]

Perhaps. But there is one other mention of Henri in Levi's memoir. In
the summer of 1944, Levi tells us, he meets an Italian civilian who provides
him with food for six months. His relationship with Lorenzo, Levi insists,
is to be distinguished emphatically from the relationship that a seducer such
as Henri has with his outside protectors.[80] Levi's vehemence is out of

character with the more measured passages of this book. His characterization of Lorenzo is startling, primarily because it is a departure from the rest of his argument concerning the nonabsolute character of finite life. It is a lapse, a lapse that may allow us to understand him better in his fallibility and to understand the ethics he struggles to achieve. He writes,

> I believe that it was really due to Lorenzo that I am alive today; and not so much for his material aid, as for his having constantly reminded me by his presence, by his natural and plain manner of being good, that there still existed a just world outside of our own, something and someone still pure and whole, not corrupt, not savage, extraneous to hatred and terror; something difficult to define, a remote possibility of good, but for which it was worth surviving.
>
> The personages in these pages are not men. Their humanity is buried, or they themselves have buried it, under an offence received or inflicted on someone else. . . . But Lorenzo was a man; his humanity was pure and uncontaminated, he was outside this world of negation. Thanks to Lorenzo, I managed not to forget that I myself was a man.[81]

Levi posits a pure good in the man who saved him. He insists that his relationship with Lorenzo is not that of a seducer but that of a "man" to another "man." It is a man-to-man relationship. The pure and uncontaminated Lorenzo, outside of this world of negation, is the inverted image of the horror of Auschwitz. He is a saint (though not Saint Sebastian). Do we need to ask why Levi protests so much, even though no one is accusing him—and if they were to accuse him, of what? Levi survived Auschwitz because he was lucky, because he adapted, because he was a skilled chemist, and because Lorenzo pitied him and allowed him the further luxury of permitting Levi to deny, to himself and to the world, that he, Primo Levi, was a seducer like Henri. And yet he may have been, if only "in embryo." Nobody's perfect.[82] Levi himself powerfully recognizes that no human condition is perfect and transforms this recognition into a saving grace. So Lorenzo is not as pure as Levi insists that he is. But if not pure, Lorenzo is at least very good. He must surely have been chastened by what he saw at Auschwitz, and when he saw this emaciated little fellow, this Primo Levi, a little guy who spoke his native tongue in the midst of a hellish Babel of language, he must surely have felt sorry for him. And he must have felt care for him. Lorenzo's pity, sorrow, and care may have preempted Levi and rescued him from assuming the place of the seducer.

That Levi wants to have nothing to do with Henri, although he would also like to know how he is, signals the uncomfortable closeness to Henri that Levi feels. Levi wastes no time in contemplating the moral position of the prominents—simple and horrible collaborators. But he agonizes over Henri. Henri *is* Levi, or, he is so close to Levi that Levi must self-consciously resist him, recognizing so much of his own carefully wrought ethos in the "perverse body" of one who is further out of the closet than himself. The need to testify comes up against the shame and the guilt of the failure of the self to be able to care in such a way as to escape the pain and the sorrow of seduction. To tell all is to admit that there is no space that we do not participate in making ourselves. Levi is far too hard on Henri because he is too hard on himself. The reclamation of one's humanity, not in the name of humanism but as a practice of the care of the self, involves such pain. That such pain is added to the horrible physical pain that is Auschwitz is tragic. But that Levi is able to feel it is amazing and tells us that the possibilities for resistance against the normalizing forces of the late modern age are much greater than we might initially think. So his harshness regarding Henri is something that should evoke in us not a feeling of pity but of a recognition that will find its fuller expression in a concern for his well-being and a hope for the easing of his torment caused by the annihilating dreams of those who wanted a perfect world, one that would have no place for people like him or Henri or Michel Foucault.

This recognition is an essential step in the process through which we might begin to practice a new art, what Foucault identified as the art "of living counter to all forms of fascism."[83] This fascism is both within us and over us. It makes our lives easy as it makes the lives of others hard. But we are never so certain as what the line between us and others is. The struggle of Primo Levi was not to determine where that line should be drawn but to find ways to erase it.

*   *   *

The ethical position enunciated by Primo Levi is a model for a modern version of the care of the self. Levi recognizes, even if he cannot accept it for himself, that the relationship of truth to freedom is mediated through seduction. Henri is a seducer, he cultivates instinctive reactions in those he seduces, but this action is not a deception. We need to be seduced into the truth that we are freer than we feel. This practice is best pursued these days by gay saints, as David Halperin attests.[84] Primo Levi is an early exemplar of the modern care for the self, someone we might admire as much for his imperfections as for his courage in the art of parrhesia. This new art has in common with the old art a concern with relationships of domination that involve varying powers, powers that are reversible and that enjoy a certain instability. But they also emerge when the care of self entails practices that must constantly confront, reshape, and reinstitute the spaces that bodies will inhabit. The power of normalization has put into question the viability of old spaces and the practices dependent upon those spaces that shaped our older selves.

So, as always, we are left to teach ourselves how to care for ourselves. The cultivation of ourselves is no exercise in narcissism but involves a deep engagement with others as we cultivate them and get them to recognize our selves in response. It is a messy process because it is a messy world. And the possibilities of change that the adoption of such an ethics proposes are not transformative but recognitive. Being free involves not simply knowing our situation but knowing how our selves are composed by the spaces we inhabit and the practices with others we engage. It is a process that must always be political not because there is no escaping domination (a world without domination is the *telos* of genocide) but because there can be no freedom in the absence of relationships of power.

Foucault has also taught us to be wary of the institutions through which we are governed. We must always beware of the possibilities that our own institutional arrangements will encourage the rise of new destructive forces inimical to the possibilities of our being free. He offers no prescriptions; he is suspicious of constitutions, of laws, of the promises of those who would insist on leading. One need not be an anarchist to share in Foucault's suspicion, even as one tries to act as a responsive and caring citizen. There is not much of a contradiction in both acting and suspecting—but potentially plenty of irony and maybe even a laugh or two. It is better to laugh than not to laugh.

Foucault has taught us that, among other things.

Notes

1. See Michel Foucault, *Discipline and Punish: The Birth of the Prison* (New York: Pantheon, 1977), 228. Here, at the conclusion of his discussion of the Panopticon, Foucault writes, "Is it any wonder that prisons resemble factories, schools, barracks, hospitals, which all resemble prisons?"

2. Several recent cases bear upon the conditions of imprisonment in the United States. The general thrust of jurisprudence has been to assert strong agentic responsibility for cruel and unusual punishment as a means of disavowing official responsibility for the conditions that bear within prisons. Unless prisoners are able to show that there is deliberate intent by wardens and guards to make conditions unbearable, they lack standing under the Fifth Amendment. See *Wilson v. Seiter,* 111 S.Ct. 2321 (1991) and *Farmer v. Brennan, Warden et al.,* 92-7247 (1994), (62LW 4446-56, June 7, 1994, *The United States Law Week,* Justice Thomas, concurring: Prisons are necessarily dangerous places; they house society's most antisocial and violent people in close proximity with one another.).

3. For a description of conditions of prison by prisoners themselves that rises to the level of literature, see Wilbert Rideau and Ron Wikberg, *Life Sentences* (New York: Times Books, 1991).

4. For a discussion of the politics of security in a disciplinary age, see Thomas L. Dumm, *united states* (Ithaca, NY: Cornell University Press, 1994), chap. 4, "Rodney King, or The New Enclosures."

5. This is perhaps the most disturbing element in the genre of popular music known as gangsta rap. What politicians are unwilling to discuss in their moralistic responses to the genre are any explanations concerning the connections these rappers are making between the experience of freedom and imprisonment. For the most striking examples of this genre see the recordings of Tupac Shakur, Snoop Doggy Dogg, Niggas with Attitude, and Dr. Dre.

6. Michel Foucault, *The History of Sexuality: Volume 1. The Will to Truth,* trans. Robert Hurley (New York: Pantheon, 1978), 139.

7. Ibid., 136.

8. Ibid.

9. Ibid., 137.

10. Ibid.

11. Ibid., 138.

12. Ibid., 138-9.

13. Ibid., 143.

14. In an essay that parallels Foucault's concerns and acknowledges the influence of Foucault's thinking about bio-power on his formulations, George Kateb suggests democratic individuality as the best safeguard against the power of normalization that results in this political capacity to risk entire populations and perhaps existence itself. See Kateb, *The Inner Ocean: Individualism and Democratic Culture* (Ithaca, NY: Cornell University Press, 1993), 123.

15. The question of the continued power of constitutional rule in the encouragement of freedom is at stake in this debate. For a defense of constitutionalism as a source of democratic legitimacy, see Kateb, *The Inner Ocean,* 57-76.

16. Foucault, *The Will to Truth,* 144.

17. Ibid.

18. Ibid. See also Foucault, "Two Lectures," in *Power\Knowledge,* ed. Colin Gordon (New York: Pantheon, 1980), 108.

19. Foucault, "Two Lectures," 108. See also Foucault, "Governmentality," in Graham Burchell, Colin Gordon, and Peter Miller, eds., *The Foucault Effect: Studies in Governmentality* (Chicago: University of Chicago Press, 1991), 102-4.

20. Foucault, "Governmentality," 104. "This state of government which bears essentially on population and both refers itself to and makes use of the economic *savoir* could be seen as corresponding to a type of society controlled by apparatuses of security."

21. The elaboration of normalization has been a major development in the work of many former students of Foucault and of his works. Among these have been the members of the editorial collective for the journal *Ideology and Consciousness,* such as Nicolas Rose and Colin Gordon, and in France, François Ewald, who is now director of the Foucault Institute. My understanding of normalization has been particularly enhanced by reading Ewald. See, for instance, "Norms, Discipline, and the Law," trans. and adapt. Marjorie Beale, in *Representations* 10 (Spring 1990).

22. Sidney Blumenthal, "The Education of a President," *The New Yorker,* 24 January 1994, 40-1.

23. Ibid., 41.

24. Ibid., my emphasis on the word *security.*

25. Michael Sandel, "Democrats and Community," *The New Republic,* 22 February 1988, 21.

26. Ibid., 23.

27. For a more detailed exploration of the shift from surveillance to monitor as a normalizing strategy, see Dumm, *united states,* chap. 4.

28. For a valuable analysis of fundamentalism, see William E. Connolly, *The Ethos of Pluralization* (Minneapolis: University of Minnesota Press, 1995), chap. 4, "Fundamentalism in America."

29. Here I again acknowledge the work of William E. Connolly, who has done more than any other political theorist in the United States to connect these concerns of Foucault to the contemporary contestations of American political culture. See esp. Connolly, *Identity\ Difference: Democratic Negotiations of Political Paradox* (Ithaca, NY: Cornell University Press, 1993). Connolly emphasizes the tensions that underlie the instabilities of identity, especially as they operate in democrat politics. Connolly's constant concern, underlined by the evolution of the American polity in this century, is its capacity to negotiate difference as identity becomes increasingly problematized in the face of normalizing practices.

30. Georges Canguilhem, "On *Histoire de la folie* as an Event," trans. Ann Hobart, *Critical Inquiry* 21 (Winter 1995): 286. Canguilhem was the third reader of Foucault's doctoral thesis, which was the text of *Historie de la folie,* later abridged and translated into English as *Madness and Civilization.* He is author of *The Normal and the Pathological* (New York: Zone Books, 1993).

31. Michel Foucault, *The History of Sexuality: Volume 3. The Care of the Self,* trans. Robert Hurley (New York: Pantheon, 1986), 239.

32. For a study that traces the emergence of this codification, see William E. Connolly, *The Augustinian Imperative: A Reflection on the Politics of Morality* (Newbury Park, CA: Sage, 1993). Connolly's exercise might be seen as a complementary volume to the unpublished fourth volume of Foucault's *The History of Sexuality, The Confessions of the Flesh.* That volume was to concern itself at least in part with Augustine.

33. This is not a universal theme of ancient practice, but Foucault suggests that it is centrally important nonetheless. See Foucault, *The History of Sexuality: Volume 2. The Use of Pleasure,* trans. Robert Hurley (New York: Pantheon, 1986), 78: "S¯ophrosyn¯e was a state that could be approached through the exercise of self-mastery and through restraint in the practice of pleasure; it was characterized as a freedom."

34. Michel Foucault, "Final Interview," trans. Thomas Levin and Isabelle Lorenz, *Raritan* 1 (Summer 1985): 3.

35. Ibid., 8. Foucault is also quite clear about the limits of learning from the Greeks in another interview. See "On the Genealogy of Ethics," in Hubert Dreyfus and Paul Rabinow, *Michel Foucault: Beyond Structuralism and Hermeneutics,* 2d ed. (Chicago: University of Chicago Press, 1983), 231-2. Here Foucault connects his project of engaging in a history of problematizations to the politics of activism. For a lengthier discussion of this project in the context of contemporary political arguments, see Thomas L. Dumm, "The Politics of Post-Modern Aesthetics," *Political Theory* 16, no. 2 (May 1988): 209-28.

36. Michel Foucault, *The Use of Pleasure,* 11.

37. Michel Foucault, *The Care of the Self,* 44. Foucault expands and elaborates on the import of this dialogue in "Technologies of the Self," in *Technologies of the Self: A Seminar with Michel Foucault,* ed. Luther Martin, Huck Gutman, and Patrick Hutton (Amherst: University of Massachusetts Press, 1988), 24-7.

38. Foucault, "Technologies of the Self," 24.

39. Ibid., 26.

40. A valuable summary of this final course is presented by Thomas Flynn. See his "Foucault as Parrhesiast: His Last Course at the Collège de France," in James Bernauer and David Rasmussen, eds., *The Final Foucault* (Cambridge: MIT Press, 1988). I rely on this summary for the following paragraph.

41. Foucault, "Technologies of the Self," 28-30. Here Foucault quotes at length from a letter by Marcus Aurelius to demonstrate the deep, if ambiguous, relationship between body and mind that emerges in this period.

42. "The Ethic of the Care for the Self as a Practice of Freedom," in Bernauer and Rasmussen, eds., *The Final Foucault, 3.*

43. Ibid., 12.

44. Ibid., 13.

45. Ibid., 18.

46. For an insightful comment on the emergence of this ethos that focuses on the "post-Auschwitz" character of this ethos, see James Bernauer, "Beyond Life and Death: On Foucault's Post-Auschwitz Ethic," in Timothy J. Armstrong, ed., *Michel Foucault: Philosopher* (New York: Routledge, 1992), esp. 268-72.

47. Michel Foucault, "What Is Enlightenment?" in Paul Rabinow, ed., *The Foucault Reader* (New York: Pantheon, 1984), 42.

48. Ibid., 42-3.

49. Ibid., 44.

50. Ibid., 45.

51. Ibid., 46.

52. Ibid., 47.

53. Ibid., 49.

54. In the United States, this sort of criticism has been focused through the lens of feminist political theory in some very interesting ways, primarily in the form of criticisms of the work of Judith Butler. I would refer the reader to Judith Butler, *Gender Trouble: Feminism and the*

Subversion of Identity (New York: Routledge, 1990), esp. her conclusion, "From Parody to Politics." Then I would urge the reader to examine an exchange between Judith Butler and Seyla Benhabib, originally in the pages of *Praxis International,* and usefully anthologized in a volume, including contributions by Nancy Fraser and Drucilla Cornell, with an introduction by Linda Nicholson, entitled *Feminist Contentions: A Philosophical Exchange* (New York: Routledge, 1995). Finally, I would refer the reader to Judith Butler, *Bodies That Matter* (New York: Routledge, 1993), esp. the introduction and the title essay, in which she elaborates on the reiterative and citational qualities of gendered identities in such a way as to refute claims that there is a "simple" desituated character to identifications.

55. Michel Foucault, "What Is Enlightenment?," 50.

56. Bernauer, "Beyond Life and Death," 271-2.

57. Ibid., 275.

58. Primo Levi, *Survival in Auschwitz,* trans. Stuart Woolf, with "A Conversation with Primo Levi by Philip Roth" (New York: Macmillan, 1960, 1986), 29.

59. Ibid., 17.

60. Ibid., 33.

61. Ibid., 41.

62. Levi writes of one incident that indicates how this process operates for those who administer the policy. He tells of Alex, his Kapo, who casually wiped his hand on Levi's shoulder:

> Without hatred and without sneering, Alex wipes his hand on my shoulder, both the palm and the back of the hand, to clean it; he would be amazed, the poor brute Alex, if someone told him that today, on the basis of this action, I judge him and Pannwitz and the innumerable others like him, large and small, in Auschwitz and everywhere. (Ibid., 107-108)

Levi retains the ability to judge, in the wake of his resistance. (One is not excluded from judging by resisting.) The capacity of the administrators of the death camps to rationalize their behavior is the source of the deepest controversies concerning explanations for Nazi death camps. I am most strongly influenced by Hannah Arendt's *Eichmann in Jerusalem: A Report on the Banality of Evil* (New York: Penguin, 1963), and Claude Lanzmann's 1985 documentary film *Shoah.*

63. Levi, *Survival in Auschwitz,* 56.

64. Ibid., 64.

65. Ibid., 9.

66. Ibid., 11.

67. *The Drowned and the Saved* is also the title of the last collection of Primo Levi's writings, trans. Raymond Rosenthal (New York: Simon & Schuster, 1988).

68. Levi, *Survival in Auschwitz,* 90.

69. Of these survivors, the "prominents" are the most common. The Jewish prominents were the worst, for Levi. These were people who accepted positions of privilege over their comrades, in return for betraying them. (Ibid., p. 91). The non-Jewish prominents were far more common, but they had not betrayed anyone; they were mere criminals recruited from prisoners to operate as supervisors in the camps.

70. Ibid., 92.

71. Ibid., 93.

72. Ibid., 94-5.

73. Ibid., 97.

74. Ibid., 98.

75. Ibid.

76. Ibid., 99.

77. Ibid., 100.

78. Ibid.

79. If one examines Sodoma's "San Sebastian" (1525, Florence), one can see his abjection. His eyes roll heavenward, seeming to see the image of an angel placing a halo upon his head: his body is feminine, pierced through the neck and legs by arrows, a loincloth delicately covering his genitalia. His skin glows. This is a painting of intense and explicit erotic beauty. That Levi compares Henri to it is telling.

80. Levi, *Survival in Auschwitz,* 119-21.

81. Ibid., 121-2.

82. Michel Foucault once addressed a group of analytic philosophers. When his host noted that Foucault had never spoken to such a group before, Foucault's response was "Nobody's perfect." The phrase operates to admit that Foucault himself makes mistakes but also that the field of analytic philosophy, which is so concerned to be perfectly precise in expression, is perhaps condemned to a particularly poignant irrelevance in an imperfect world. (William E. Connolly told me this story, so it must be true, but then again, nobody's perfect.)

83. Michel Foucault, "Preface," to Gilles Deleuze and Félix Guatarri, *Anti-Oedipus: Capitalism and Schizophrenia,* trans. Robert Hurey, Mark Seem, and Helen R. Lane (Minneapolis: University of Minnesota Press, 1983), xiii.

84. See David Halperin, *Saint Foucault: Toward a Gay Hagiography* (New York: Oxford University Press, 1995).

Index

About the Author

Thomas L. Dumm is Associate Professor in the Political Science Department at Amherst College, where he teaches courses in American politics and contemporary political thought. His earlier books include *Democracy and Punishment: Disciplinary Origins of the United States* (1987) and *united states* (1994). He also has coedited, with Frederick Dolan, *Rhetorical Republic: Governing Representations in American National Politics* (1993). He is currently completing a study of contemporary punishment in the United States, *The Penitentiary in Ruins*, which will include documentary photographs by Jonathan Crispin and Michael Jacobson-Hardy. He is also beginning a study of solitude and the politics of isolation in late modern life.